# TRUMPOCALYPSE
# NOW!

## The Triumph of the
## Conspiracy Spectacle

# Kenn Thomas

Adventures Unlimited Press

**Trumpocalypse Now!**

by Kenn Thomas

ISBN 978-1-939149-78-7

Published by:
Adventures Unlimited Press
One Adventure Place
Kempton, Illinois  60946  USA
auphq@frontiernet.net

www.AdventuresUnlimitedPress.com

Printed in the United States of America

# TRUMPOCALYPSE NOW!

## The Triumph of the Conspiracy Spectacle

Adventures Unlimited Press

"Donald Trump is here tonight. Now, I know that he's taken some flak lately, but no one is prouder to put this birth certificate matter to rest than The Donald. And that's because he can finally get back to focusing on the issues that matter, like, did we fake the moon landing? What really happened in Roswell? And where are Biggie and Tupac?"

—President Barack Obama
at the White House Correspondent's Dinner
April 29, 2011

# TABLE OF CONTENTS

Additional AUP titles by Kenn Thomas:

*NASA, Nazis and JFK*
*Mind Control, Oswald and JFK*
*Popular Paranoia*
*Inside the Gemstone File*
*Parapolitics: Conspiracy In Contemporary America*

# TRUMPOCALYPSE NOW!

## The Triumph of the Conspiracy Spectacle

## Kenn Thomas

The dragon stood on the shore of the sea. And I saw a beast coming out of the sea. It had ten horns and seven heads, with ten crowns on its horns, and on each head a blasphemous name. The beast I saw resembled a leopard, but had feet like those of a bear and a mouth like that of a lion. The dragon gave the beast his power and his throne and great authority. One of the heads of the beast seemed to have had a fatal wound, but the fatal wound had been healed. The whole world was filled with wonder and followed the beast. People worshiped the dragon because he had given authority to the beast, and they also worshiped the beast and asked, "Who is like the beast? Who can wage war against it?"

*– Revelations 13*

# Foreword

# by Robert Sterling

"The horror. The horror."
—Marlon Brando as Colonel Kurtz
in Francis Ford Coppola's *Apocalypse Now*

It is perhaps fitting the first words in this political tome were among the few mumbled half-coherently by Brando in Coppola's cinematic masterpiece. (Although, if you want to get literary, it must be noted they were directly lifted from Joseph Conrad's *Heart of Darkness* original source material.) And it's fitting not merely due to both Brando's Kurtz and Trump being paranoid autocrats whose pathos leads them to bark increasingly nonsensical and delusional orders. It is fitting in part because this book, like the film before it, both reference an Apocalypse in the title, as both Vietnam and the 2016 election are true revelations on the nature of American society. Perhaps more so, it is fitting because *Apocalypse Now* is in that special group of films, primarily from the 1970s and 80s (a canon which would also include the likes of Martin Scorsese's *Taxi Driver* and Stanley Kubrick's *The Shining*) where tales of violent shock were mixed with more than a splash of dark humor to the point where the line between horror and absurdist comedy become blurred. In the election of Donald Trump to the White House, the horror and absurdity of modern politics has reached a zenith. (Well, at least for now.)

The punchline is that Trump has long been a punchline himself for the banality of modern times. He first gained notoriety in the eighties as a self-promoting real estate tycoon in New York's landscape. He was a blowhard of epic proportions, outpacing the likes of Lee Iacocca and Jack Welch in the competitive field of self-aggrandizement. He soon earned the devoted wrath of many, most notably *Spy Magazine*, which labeled him "a short-fingered vulgarian" and chose bashing Trump as their raison d'etre. *Spy*, a highly influential satirical monthly founded in 1986 that inspired many a writer, saw in The Donald a symbol of everything that was wrong with the shameless greed of the Reagan years. *Spy*'s relentless bashing of Trump culminated in what many assumed to be his deserved demise when Trump's empire appeared ready to collapse in the early nineties. The general view at this humiliating moment for Trump was that while he spent the eighties bragging about his business prowess, the true business innovators like Bill Gates, Sam Walton and Warren Buffet were quietly but efficiently revolutionizing computers, retail and investment.

Trump was certainly down for much of the nineties, but he was never out. The decade could best be described as his "John Lennon on heroin" era. Of course, Donald being Donald, Trump wasn't content merely laying around the house shooting up smack like the former Beatle. Trump was still an unapologetic tabloid headline chaser, with tales of his marriages and divorces to both Ivana Trump and Marla Maples dominating eyeballs at the supermarket checkout aisles. To his credit, Trump endured those years of struggle and came out even more successful by the end of the millennium. Incidentally, *Spy Magazine* ceased publishing in 1998.

Trump's comeback went to another level when he became host of *The Apprentice*. The show became a success, and he became a noted figure in the inane field of Reality Television dreck. (Considering that Reality TV includes such noted brain rot as Paris Hilton, the Kardashians and Temptation Island, this is an impressive achievement.) Still, for all his success—which also included owning the Miss USA and Miss Universe beauty pageants, along with numerous hotels, casinos and golf courses with his last name affixed to the title—he was still viewed publicly as more of an entertaining buffoon than a respectable businessman, and when he first announced his presidential campaign, it was dismissed by many in the press as a publicity prank. The *Huffington Post* even listed all articles on his campaign in the entertainment section of the news site.

This makes his victory all the more surreal. Some even cite it as proof (along with the death of Nelson Mandela and the spelling of Berenstain Bears) that our universe is a computer simulation now experiencing extreme glitches. Trump's trip to the White House has been as long and strange as that of the most devoted of Deadhead, although as improbable as it seems, it was indeed predicted in a 2000 episode of *The Simpsons* (which included it as an preposterous joke.) What makes this even stranger is how he did it by embracing conspiracy theories like no mainstream candidate before him. (Sorry, Lyndon Larouche, you don't count.) Granted, the right-wing has long championed conspiracy theory (provided the theory has been distilled of any ideologically threatening elements) to promote its cause. Jonathan Vankin devoted an entire chapter of his essential 1991 book *Conspiracies, Cover-Ups and Crimes* to how the right uses conspiratorial thought for political advantage, and in 1964, Richard Hofstadter wrote an acclaimed essay for *Harper Magazine* titled "The Paranoid Style in American Politics" to explain the rise of Barry Goldwater. Still, for every John Bircher grumble of PBS being part of the communist menace, up to the modern day suspicion that Barack Obama is a Kenya-born radical Muslim socialist, the GOP establishment has long kept an arm's length from this political fringe, so it could simultaneously appear as reasonable while benefiting from less respectable fellow travelers.

There is no distance between Trump and this fringe: his Chief Strategist, Steve Bannon, previously ran the ultra-right *Breitbart News*, which gained notoriety for peddling in paranoid parapolitics. Perhaps even more infamous is his bromance with Infowars website owner and radio host (as well as Bill Hicks lookalike) Alex Jones. Jones, a man whose carnival barker style conceals a sharp mind and an astute business sense, has become the mainstream media's face for modern day conspiracy thought, and he has been an ardent supporter of Trump, who has been a frequent guest of his show. Considering Trump is now Commander in Chief, one could argue now is the moment of supremacy of conspiracy culture in America. Making that supremacy even more telling is the Democratic Party's reaction to the Trump movement, ascribing it to a nefarious Russian plot by the sinister Vladimir Putin to "hack" our elections and install a Manchurian candidate in the White House.

The "Trump is a Russian mole" is amusingly ironic, because as it turns out, Trump's most obvious political influence is Roy Cohn. Cohn, one of the more repulsive individuals of the 20th century, was the right hand man and top henchman of Joseph McCarthy during the Communist witch hunt where he ruthlessly accused others of being Soviet agents. Cohn was also, from 1971 until his death in 1986, a close confidant of Trump, becoming a mentor to The Donald. This is one of those facts that, once learned, is hard to ignore. Whatever the differences in substance between the two men, it becomes obvious in Trump's manner and style that he is mirroring the aggressive and bullying tendencies of Cohn.

The influence of Cohn explains so much more of Trump. For one, Cohn was notorious for not paying his bills, using his formidable legal skills to evade payments that were owed. (To his credit, the closeted yet venomously homophobic Cohn would at least pay all balances due to male prostitutes he hired.) Cut to Trump, and what is his modus operandi? Stiffing people again and again, whether they be banks, contractors, or (oftentimes) workers. The repetition is so blatant, it becomes hard to believe so many working class voters put their faith in a real estate salesman with a history of screwing his employees and who is known for his catchphrase "You're fired."

Hard to believe, but it becomes understandable in context. While the mainstream press has received deserved contempt in the Trump era, journalist Salena Zito seemed to astutely observe his appeal in September 2016. Writing in *The Atlantic*, she put it succinctly: "The press takes him literally, but not seriously; his supporters take him seriously, but not literally."

In politics, comparing someone to Hitler is the equivalent of rushing the net at Wimbledon: it's an easy way to end things quickly and usually in your favor. Trump isn't immune to the Hitler charges, and rightfully so. Still, the apt comparison is truthful in ways which lead to inconvenient truths. Say what you want about the tenets of National Socialism, you don't have to be a Nazi to think Germany got a raw deal from the Treaty of Versailles, or that the Weimar Republic seemed ineffective in helping a German working class battered first by hyperinflation in the 1920s and then by mass depression the 1930s. If Trump is Hitler in this comparison, then Barack Obama is certainly Hindenburg (the political leader, although the blimp named after him is another deserved metaphor). In 2009, Obama entered the White House with massive public support and a decided majority in both chambers of Congress, including a veto-proof sixty votes in the Senate. The US faced its greatest economic crisis since the Great Depression, pushed by Wall Street greed that would make Ivan Boesky blush, and the time seemed ripe for a second New Deal. Instead of a New Deal, "Yes We Can" Obama gave the public eight years of the same neoliberal crap the Democratic Party has been pushing since the Reagan era.

Two of the few guys who smelled something rotten were Michael Moore and radio host Jimmy Dore, and their warnings were proven prophetic. In the northern industrial states of Michigan, Pennsylvania and Wisconsin, huge numbers of working class voters felt helpless and battered during the eight years preceding the 2016 election. Like the Weimar Republic's focus on culture and arts that many viewed as increasingly depraved, Obama seemed less interested in the plight of the working class than he was in protecting the choice of bathroom by teenage transgenders. Instead of dealing with issues of economic inequality and mass poverty, the "liberal" establishment focused more on the worst of identity politics, dismissing any concerns of modern society that couldn't be reduced to race, sex, sexual orientation or sexual identity. White working males, rather than viewed as victims of neoliberal economics, were dismissed as privileged oppressors who had no reason to bitch about anything. What if people still cried about their economic plight? Obama would sniff indifferently, then point to the obviously creepy Republicans, and pretty much dare people to vote for the GOP if they didn't like what the Democratic Party was delivering.

I'll admit, I neither voted for Trump nor took his campaign too seriously, as he seemed too much of a jackass for the public to embrace. But in retrospect, I did see the writing on the wall long ago. In 2010, seeing the dismal response by the Democratic Party to the economic crisis that America faced, the parallels to the 1930s were too obvious. I wrote to quite a few of my friends and family members at the time that our system could not last where it was heading, and that we would either get a reform that comes from the left, like the United States did with FDR, or one from the right, like it did in Italy and Germany.

In this sense, the decision of the masses in 2016 becomes understandable. The left had their option in Bernie Sanders, an option that was decisively blocked by the Democratic Party establishment. What the left was left with was Hillary Clinton, a woman with a lack of warmth that failed to conceal she wasn't going to deviate from the neoliberal agenda. She even used the same lame uninspired rhetoric of Obama (sans his admitted charisma). Instead of bitter clingers to guns, religion and "antipathy to people who aren't like them as a way to explain their frustrations," voters got the even more pleasant "basket of deplorables" moniker from Clinton to dismiss their anger. Faced with this, many voters took Obama's dare and voted for Trump. Even after defeat, with all the Russia-baiting, the Democrats sounded more comfortable (and a lot more sincere) copying the rhetoric of McCarthy rather than that of FDR and the New Deal.

All this is why, even if this moment is a victory for the conspiracy culture, it is a pyrrhic victory at best. When the conspiracy culture exploded in the nineties from the germ founded by the likes of Mae Brussell before, it was (at least at its best) about challenging ideas about history, society and, indeed, existence itself. Conspiracy theorizing can turn into a game (and that's not a bad thing) and sometimes even the best can engage in dot-connecting to where it becomes ridiculous, but even at that extreme it can be a healthy exercise of mind expansion. The conspiratorial currents Trump peddles in are not about expanding the mind, but rather reducing thought to obedience to a megalomaniac narcissist. The effect of this can be seen in Alex Jones, who for all his flaws, was once a sharp thinker behind his Andy Kaufman performance art. Now, his conspiracy rants have devolved to the lowest common denominator, and he is a flunky to Trump so pathetically, Trump would be trading his anus for cigarettes if they were both in prison. (It must be said that Jones is much more wealthy and powerful for his Faustian pact, so all is not completely lost.) Of course, the devolved nature of conspiracy culture goes beyond Jones, which explains the inordinate time 4Chan and Reddit users have devoted looking at Instagram photos for proof Hillary runs a cannibalistic child-sacrificing Satanic cult beneath a DC pizza parlor.

And this is why, whatever the future holds for Trump, the future doesn't look good. Trump is but the symptom, and the pathology is still there. Trump may remain too in your face for the establishment to swallow, but the establishment, as always, is desperate to legitimize the powerful. Before Trump turned the GOP primary into a pro wrestling match, they were as eager to embrace Jeb Bush (or any other candidate the square community could get behind) as much as they embraced Hillary. It seems like it's only a matter of time before another Donald Trump comes around, only next time the establishment will unite behind and cheer for him.

# Chapter 1

# "Alternative Facts"

*I'm sentimental if you know what I mean*
*I love the country but I can't stand the scene*
*And I'm neither left or right*
*I'm just sitting home tonight*
*Getting lost in that hopeless little screen*
—Leonard Cohen (9/21/1934-11/7/2016)

Presidential counselor Kellyanne Conway struck a responsive chord at the start of the Trump era when she referred to comments from the new president's press secretary—deemed false by the majority press—as "alternative facts." At issue was the size of the presidential inaugural. During his first briefing with members of the media, press secretary Sean Spicer maintained that the event had the "largest audience to ever witness an inauguration," despite statistical data and even aerial photography that showed evidence to the contrary.

More than just awkward phraseology or a slip of the tongue, the phrase amounted to an ideological declaration. Trump himself had led his march to the White House with a long line of similar alternative facts: "birtherism," promoting the rumor that Barack Obama was not born in the United States, and then claiming that the rumor was started by his own political opposition; that his Christianity made him a target for tax auditing; that vaccines caused autism; that climate change doesn't exist; that the 9/11 plane crashes were cheered by thousands in the streets of New Jersey; many claims involving immigrants and immigration; and that one of his political opponents was involved with the JFK assassination.

These alternative facts and many like them had preceded

Donald Trump's campaign for many years. That mainstream media sources howled in laughter at them was nothing new either. The major corporate media had long been aggravated by a growing body of independent researchers and scholars who arrived at conclusions at odds with what TV, radio and newspaper news delivered to their homes daily. Donald Trump was just another conspiracy theorist, a category that provided the foundation for a culture of ridicule perpetrated in the mainstream. That very culture of ridicule, in fact, was offered by pundits as the reason for Donald Trump's success in the 2016 presidential race, or at the very least, why major news sources had it so totally wrong in their predictions about the election.

Trump was only the latest celebrity to have tapped into the conspiracy culture. Political figures like the former governor of Minnesota Jesse Ventura, and entertainment celebrities like actor Will Smith and comedian Richard Belzer, had long added the sobriquet "conspiracy theorist" to their publicity materials. It was exotic and it suggested advanced knowledge and independent thought. The top-down model of mass media communication also had long been eroded, first by the Internet and then by the social media superimposed on that architecture. Straight conspiracy chatter became mixed up with dating social media. Facebook and Twitter, became the new favored direct line of communication between Trump's White House and the people. Not only had the line between conspiracy and celebrity been blurred but with Trump it had been smeared into power politics. The spectacle that conspiracy theories had become had now achieved actual power.

Yet, a greater phenomenon remained under the glare of the spectacle, the actual parapolitical underground, the world of Mae Brussels and John Judge and many other independent scholars who eschewed and were marginalized by the large corporate news services. This was a world that Trump and other conspiracy celebrities emulated but rarely referred to, a world of serious scholars without political ambitions and coming from the full left-right spectrum of opinion. Even as the Trump camp and the mainstream media developed a new false dialogue for a new administration, the smart observers, the real conspiracy theorists, set about putting current events into a more authentic historical and parapolitical context.

Affirmation of this came when Dan Rather, the former CBS news anchor, responded to Kellyanne Conway's alternative facts remark. "These are not normal times. These are extraordinary times. And extraordinary times call for extraordinary measures.," he blogged ominously. "When you have a spokesperson for the president of the United States wrap up a lie in the Orwellian phrase 'alternative facts' …when you have a press secretary in his first appearance before the White House reporters threaten, bully, lie and then walk out of the briefing room without the *cajones* to answer a single question…" Rather said, describing the circumstances of that first press conference. "Facts and the truth are not partisan," he went on, "they are the bedrock of democracy. And you are either with them, with us, with Our Constitution, our history, and the future of all our nation, or you are against it. Everyone must answer that question."

If the times did not appear normal to Rather they may have seemed familiar. Rather had long been widely known in conspiracy circles for an alternate fact of his own: that when JFK was shot his head "went forward with considerable violence." Rather repeated that description a number of times in television and radio interviews shortly after the assassination and long before the infamous Zapruder film of JFK's murder had been seen by the general public. (Researcher Robert Groden and comedian/philosopher Dick Gregory first brought the Z film to national television on Geraldo Rivera's *Good Night America* show on March 6, 1975.) This description had for many years provided support for the lone gunman theory of the assassination, since a bullet moving Kennedy's head in that direction could only have come from behind, from the school book depository. The lone gunman theory has been widely discredited among students of the assassination and the wide availability of the Z film has long demonstrated that the president's head moves backward with considerable violence, the opposite of Rather's description.

Without getting into too many arcane details about the JFK assassination—although it did come to play an important role in Donald Trump's political campaign (see chapter 6)—Rather's reaction underscores a reality about Trump's "alternative facts," if not his political success itself. It is not the product of the traditional partisan divide. Trump vanquished the politicians typically associated with conspiratorial manipulations, like the Bush family, and decimated traditional GOP ranks during the political primaries of 2016. He brought along many more alternative notions of conspiracy—Obama birtherism, 9/11 plots, Clinton conspiracies, votescam suspicions—not from studied, respected sources, but from Internet chatter, rumor and a half-perceived, half created world of his own. It was a campaign not of serious left-right political debate but one of spectacle, with Trump accruing valuable TV time free as the ultimate conspiracy celebrity.

At the same time, Trump brought with him to the White House parapolitical intrigue of his own. Despite his campaign promise, he never released his tax returns, even after his excuse about being audited was exhausted, leaving open extensive speculation concerning his global financial entanglements and the long histories of conspiratorial activity they may reflect. His involvements with Russia and Russian involvement with cyber hacking and subverting the primary process of the Democratic Party have left open wide areas of study for future students of parapolitics.

Kellyanne Conway came to the Trump campaign from that of one of his primary rivals, Ted Cruz, the man Trump associated with the JFK assassination. As she began to evolve the concept of "alternative facts" to one of "alternative information," she attempted to defend the then current attempt by her boss to impose travel restrictions on seven countries he regarded as Islamo-terrorist threats. She claimed this effort was in part inspired by a massacre that took place in Bowling Green, Kentucky. No such massacre occurred. Instead, a pair of Iraqi refugees had been arrested in Bowling Green in 2011 on charges involving their attempts to provide material support to al Qaeda in Iraq and supporting attacks on US troops. Enterprising symapticos took up donations for victims of the nonexistent Bowling Green massacre and vigils were held in two states. Conway later apologized for characterizing the Bowling Green arrests as a massacre, stating that, "Frankly they were terrorists in Bowling Green but their massacre took place in Iraq."

The idea of alternative facts has been traced to the ghostwritten autobiography of Donald Trump, *The Art of the Deal* (Random House, 1987). Its alternate author, Tony Schwarz, coined the term "truthful hyperbole," which he characterized as innocent exaggeration and a "very effective form of promotion." Schwartz maintained, "people want to believe that something is the biggest and the greatest and the most spectacular". This is almost the reverse of conspiracy theory, where people believe the darkest, most sinister idea to be the most spectacular. That dialectic has come to characterize the beginning of the Trump era.

**TRUMPOCALYPSE REVELATIONS:**
**An Alternate Inauguration**

Sixty nine Democrats did not attend
Dozens of celebrities refused to perform
Many unclaimed free tickets to the event
Twenty eight protest groups at the National Mall
200 protesters arrested; protest events in all 50 states
Number of inaugural balls reduced to three
Million dollar donations solicited for access during the inauguration
89-year-old inauguration announcer Charles Brotman, announcer for the event since 1957, fired by Trump
A light turnout, demonstrated in photographs and misrepresented by White House press secretary Sean Spicer, leads to Kellyanne Conway's observation about "alternate facts"

## TRUMPOCALYPSE REVELATIONS:
## A Calendar of Trump Administration
## Highlights

January 2017
1/20
Begins issuing infamous executive orders:
Freezes the creation new federal regulations
Suspends rate cuts for homeowners insurance
Signs "ease the burden" order to start the repeal of
Obamacare Affordable Care Act health insurance

1/21
Millions join the Women's March on Washington in cities
throughout the US

1/23
Freezes federal hiring
Withdraws from Trans-Pacific Partnership
Stops US funds provided to international health clinics
that provide abortion counseling

1/24
Restarts Dakota Access and Canadian Keystone XL oil
pipelines

1/25
Orders more immigration detention centers and
enforcement personnel
Defunds the federal money from sanctuary cities, which
do not prosecute undocumented immigrants
Orders work to begin on a new southern border wall
between the US and Mexico

1/27
Expands security checks for foreign nationals
Limits the number of refugees allowed into the US and
suspends entry from seven countries (Yemen, Syria,
Somalia, Libya, Sudan, Iraq and Iran). This action resulted
in a lawsuit from the State of Washington that upheld a
restraining order against it.
Orders reassessment of American military and nuclear
resources

1/28
Reorganizes National Security Council, adding strategist
Steve Bannon

1/30
Adds the CIA to the National Security Council
Orders that every new federal business regulation be
accompanied by the removal of two existing regulations
Fires acting Attorney General Sally Yates after she directs
Justice Department lawyers not to defend the directives on
immigration travel ban; appoints Dana Boente

1/31
Nominates Neil McGill Gorsuch to Supreme Court

# Chapter 2

# Conspiracy Celebrity

"In societies dominated by modern conditions of production,
life is presented as an immense accumulation of spectacles.
Everything that was directly lived has receded into a
representation."

—Guy Debord, *Society of the Spectacle*

Much of Donald Trump's fame comes from his career in television spectacle. Like another politician—cum—conspiracy theorist, former Minnesota governor Jesse Ventura, some of Trump's earlier renown comes from his association with TV wrestling. He served as a host and guest for various *Wrestlemania* events. These events, of course, involve very little actual wrestling or any other type of sport. Rather, they retain the extracted essence of spectacle from the real thing and exist primarily as promotional vehicles for ersatz wrestling celebrities. Trump continued with this activity well past 2013, when he was inducted into the World Wrestling Federation's Hall of Fame in Madison Square Garden.

Trump first hosted a *Wrestlemania* event in 1988, the same year he first thought of running for president, according to his biography. At the time he was embroiled in debts accruing to the Taj Mahal casino. He actually made his first formal bid for the White House on the Reform Party ticket in the year 2000. Fifteen thousand people voted for him in that party's California primary. Trump considered the idea of running for president again in 2004 and 2012. In between and following those inclinations he considered efforts to run for the office of New York's governor. Many suspected that these inclinations to run amounted to little more than rumors planted in order to promote his television show *The Apprentice.*

The only Reform Party candidate ever to win a major office, of course, was the aforementioned wrestler, Jesse Ventura. Ventura became governor of Minnesota in 1999 after winning a narrow and unexpected political victory. Known as "The Body," Ventura too "fought" in the "professional" wrestling world of faux competition for eleven years, from 1975 to 1986. Donald Trump first hosted a *Wrestlemania* event in 1988, remarkably like a tag—team partner to Jesse "The Body" Ventura.

The other abiding similarity between the two men: conspiracy theories. Actual conspiracy haunted politics in Minnesota. The US senator who represented that state, Paul Wellstone, died in a plane crash a week and a half before the 2002 election he was favored to win. In the previous election of 2000, Missouri's governor Mel Carnahan died in a similarly mysterious plane crash. This all happened in the context of a rising right—wing parapolitical tide that included the controversial voting recount that ended with George W. Bush attaining the presidency in 2001. Governor Ventura's only real interest in all of this came during a memorial service for Wellstone, when he objected to a speech given by a friend of Wellstone's. He had intended to replace Wellstone with another Democrat but his view of what he saw as a left— politicized memorial changed his mind and instead he appointed someone from the Independent Party. The rightist media, including Rush Limbaugh and Alex Jones, echoed Ventura's opinions in this regard and perhaps shaped them.

Proud of his independent thinking, conspiracy theories percolated in Jesse Ventura's public profile. He brought up controversies surrounding 9/11, including the stand—down theory (that NORAD jets were ordered to stand—down as the 9/11/ attacks took place); that explosives destroyed the buildings, not planes; and that the catastrophe was staged as a false flag event. Later, Trump would become embroiled in 9/11 controversies of his own. Questions about this and similar things reached their full expression for Ventura with the creation of his television show

*Conspiracy Theory* in late 2009.

Donald Trump's most noted accomplishment on television, of course, came in the form of the television show *The Apprentice*. *The Apprentice* presented a premise as false as professional wrestling: people competed for the boss' favor and were dismissed when he deemed them inadequate. No actual workers were hired or fired, just as no actual wrestlers actually competed. *Apprentice* began in 2003, with a celebrity version starting the following year. Trump remained associated until he too was "fired" in June 2015 for the bad publicity his comments about immigrants attracted. He was replaced by former California governor and former WWF supporter Arnold Schwarzenegger.

The choice of Schwarzenegger as a replacement came as no small cause of consternation to Trump. Although he abandoned *The Apprentice* for the sake of his presidential campaign, the trouble he had letting go of the connection became a prime example of Trump's misplaced priorities. Instead of attending to affairs of state, Trump's attention turned to a macho competition about the show's ratings. "Wow, the ratings are in and Arnold Schwarzenegger got swamped (or destroyed) by comparison to the ratings machine… So much for being a movie star—and that was season 1 compared to season 14. Now compare him to my season 1. But who cares, he supported Kasich & Hillary." It became basic macho competition via Twitter, more a continuation of WWF than *Apprentice*.

Was it a competition for who was the bigger, badder Nazi? Schwarzenegger had long been regarded among conspiratologists in his state as the son of an SS Nazi officer and an admirer of Hitler. His dictatorial ambitions were cut short only by his ineligibility to run for Trump's office. Schwarzenegger had, in fact, remained loyal to Kurt Waldheim, the former secretary general of the United Nations who was exposed as having participated as a Nazi soldier in the mass murder atrocities in the Kozora region of western Bosnia. Waldheim was, in fact, wanted by the War Crimes Commission of the United Nations long prior to his becoming head of that organization. Arnold Schwarzenegger supported and campaigned for Waldheim in Waldheim's successful bid for president of Austria in 1986. A month after Waldheim's Nazi past became exposed, he sent a wedding gift to Schwarzenegger and Maria Shriver, whose family tree also reverberated with Nazi connections. Schwarzenegger's note in response: "My friends don't want me to mention Kurt's name, because of all the recent Nazi stuff and the U. N. controversy, but I love him and Maria does too, and so thank you."

These controversies appeared farther back in the past than Donald Trump apparently was able to or had any desire to reach. He just didn't like Schwarzenegger replacing him on his old TV spectacle. In response to Trump's twitter tantrum, the former California governor told the press: "I said let's sit on it for an hour. I called my assistant and said I think what we really should do is request a meeting and go back to New York. And then we just smash his face into a table."

Arnold Schwarzenegger left *Celebrity Apprentice* after a single season because of low ratings, much to Donald Trump's delight. Upon leaving he thanked the various celebrities and the TV show's crew saying he would love to work with them again on a show "that doesn't have this baggage."

This kind of tawdry TV spectacle became the first lesson of the Trump presidential win, an entirely new pathway to political power. In addition to *The Apprentice*, the various Miss Universe pageants and Miss USA contests, Trump had long been a cartoon cameo in television shows like *Spin City* and movies like *Zoolander*. In an episode of the *Simpsons* from March 2000 entitled "Bart to the Future," the brat Bart dreams of his sister Lisa becoming president after a Trump term of office that has bankrupted the country. The show's writer told the press, "What we needed was for Lisa to have problems that were beyond her fixing, that everything went as bad as it possibly could, and that's' why we had Trump be president before her."

That kind of derision accompanied most headlines in the daily New York press as Trump's campaign began to take shape. A *New York Post* headline read "Don Voyage!" and the *Daily News* declared "Clown Runs For Prez," replete with a photo of Trump in clown white makeup and nose. The culture of ridicule continued on to the nightly talk shows, with even Trump's staunchest opponents, the likes of comedians Steve Colbert and Jon Stewart, unable to do anything but gather attention for their foil. That, in turn, became a microcosm of the major corporate media, which could not turn its cameras away from the candidate, saving him the expense of a typical campaign.

## TRUMPOCALYPSE REVELATIONS
## A DONALD TRUMP VIDEOGRAPHY

2008—2017 The Apprentice (TV Series)
— I Don't Have Time for Anyone's Ego Except My Own (2017) ... (executive producer)
— Bon Voyage (2017) ... (executive producer)
— I'm Going Full Ballmer (2017) ... (executive producer)
— Scissors and Some Creativity (2017) ... (executive producer)
— Candy for a Billionaire (2017) ... (executive producer)
2014 Miss Universe 2014 (TV Special) (executive producer)
2013 Miss Universe 2013 (TV Special) (executive producer)
2012 Miss Universe 2012 (TV Special) (executive producer)
2012 The 2012 Miss USA Pageant (TV Special) (executive producer — as Donald Trump)
2010 The 2010 Miss Universe Pageant (TV Special) (executive producer)
2010 Donald J. Trump Presents: The Ultimate Merger (TV Series documentary) (executive producer — as Donald Trump)
2009 Miss Universe Pageant (TV Special) (executive producer — as Donald Trump)

2009 Miss USA 2009 (TV Special) (executive producer — as Donald Trump)

2009 The Girls of Hedsor Hall (TV Series) (executive producer — 2 episodes)

— Etiquette (2009) … (executive producer — as Donald Trump)

— Assessment and Appearance (2009) … (executive producer — as Donald Trump)

2008 The 57th Annual Miss USA Pageant (TV Special) (executive producer — as Donald Trump)

2007 Pageant Place (TV Series) (executive producer — 1 episode)

— After the Fall (2007) … (executive producer — as Donald Trump)

2006 Miss USA 2006 (TV Special) (producer)

2005 The Apprentice: Martha Stewart (TV Series) (executive producer — as Donald Trump)

2005 Miss Universe 2005 (TV Special) (executive producer — as Donald Trump)

2003 Miss Universe Pageant (TV Special) (executive producer — as Donald Trump)

2002 Miss Universe Pageant (TV Special) (executive producer — as Donald Trump)

2002 Miss USA 2002 (TV Special) (executive producer — as Donald Trump)

2001 Miss Universe 2001 (TV Special documentary) (executive producer — as Donald Trump)


2015 The 2000's: A New Reality (TV Mini—Series)
Interviewee (as Donald Trump)

2011 Horrorween
Forbes Cover Billionaire (as Donald Trump)

2004 Marmalade
Donald Trump (as Donald Trump)

2002 Two Weeks Notice
Donald Trump (as Donald Trump)

2002 Donald Trump's Real Estate Tycoon! (Video Game)
Donald Trump (voice)
2002 Monk (TV Series)
— Mr. Monk and the Psychic (2002) ... Men in the party
(uncredited)
2001 Zoolander
Donald Trump (as Donald Trump)
1999 Sex and the City (TV Series)
— The Man, the Myth, the Viagra (1999) ... Donald Trump
(uncredited)
1998 Sabrina, the Teenage Witch (TV Series)
— Good Will Haunting (1998) ... Daniel Ray McLeech
(uncredited)
1998 Celebrity
Donald Trump (as Donald Trump)
1998 54
VIP Patron (as Donald Trump)
1998 Spin City (TV Series)
— The Paul Lassiter Story (1998) ... Donald Trump (as
Donald Trump)
1997 NightMan (TV Series)
— Face to Face (1997) ... Donald Trump (as Donald Trump)
— Whole Lotta Shakin'... (1997) ... Donald Trump
(uncredited)
1997 The Drew Carey Show (TV Series)
— New York and Queens (1997) ... Donald Trump (as
Donald Trump)
1997 Suddenly Susan (TV Series)
— I'll See That and Raise You Susan (1997) ... Donald
Trump (as Donald Trump)
1996 The Associate
Donald Trump (uncredited)
1996 The Nanny (TV Series)
Donald Trump
— The Rosie Show (1996) ... Donald Trump (as Donald
Trump)

1996 Eddie

Donald Trump (as Donald Trump)

1995 Across the Sea of Time

Donald Trump (as Donald Trump)

1994 The Little Rascals

Waldo's Dad (as Donald Trump)

1994 The Fresh Prince of Bel—Air (TV Series)

— For Sale by Owner (1994) ... Donald Trump (as Donald Trump)

1993 The Pickle

Donald Trump (uncredited)

1992 Home Alone 2: Lost in New York

Donald Trump (as Donald Trump)

1989 Ghosts Can't Do It

Donald Trump (as Donald Trump)

1981—1985 The Jeffersons (TV Series)

— You'll Never Get Rich (1985) ... Donald Trump (uncredited)

— My Hero (1981) ... Donald Trump (uncredited)

Donald Trump as depicted on *The Simpsons*.

# Chapter 3

# Birtherism

"Birtherism" refers to the effort to discredit the legitimacy of Barack Obama's presidency due to the notion held by some that he was not born in the United States. The US Constitution, article 2, forbids anyone but a natural born citizen of the country to hold the office. More precisely, article two reads: "No person except a natural born citizen, or a citizen of the United States, at the time of this adoption of the Constitution, shall be eligible to the office of president; neither shall any person be eligible to that office which shall not have attained to the age of thirty five years, and been fourteen years a resident within the United States." That Barack Obama violated this article became the conspiracy theory with the highest profile in Donald Trump's bid for the presidency.

Historically, presidential eligibility requirements were amended twice under article II, neither change having to do with this requirement of natural birth on American soil. Back in 1804 an amendment had extended the requirements of article to the office of the vice presidency. In 1951 anyone who held the office for two terms became ineligible to hold it for another.

Three versions of birtherism circulated. One argued that Obama was not a natural born US citizen but had a dual American-British citizenship. Another claimed that he lost his US citizenship when he became a citizen of Indonesia as a child. Most prominent of the theories, however, claimed that he was not born in the United States at all but rather he was born in Kenya. Critics of these theories considered them based on racist resentment over America's first president of African American descent.

Such challenges did not come without antecedents in history, however. Upon the 1881 assassination of James Garfield, the twentieth US president, birther questions arose about his successor, Chester Arthur. Officially born in Fairfield, Vermont, political opponents asserted, but never proved, that he was born in Canada—and of one Irish parent. In 1916 a supporter of Woodrow Wilson made unproven claims that Wilson's opponent, defeated by a slim margin, actually had been born in Wales, despite his claim of birth in Glens Falls, New York.

Birther controversy attended the 1964 presidential campaign of Barry Goldwater. Goldwater came into the word in 1909 in Arizona, then a territory, not a state. That he was born in an incorporated territory kept the issue from gaining any traction. The parents of 1968 presidential candidate George Romney, Mitt's father, also were born in a territory prior to statehood, Utah. They chose US citizenship for their son, who nevertheless was actually born in Chihuahua, Mexico, at a Mormon colony. The complexities of that origin story had little impact on the election.

Legal challenges to the eligibility of 2008 presidential candidate John McCain ended with the senate passing a non-binding resolution in the affirmative for McCain. McCain was born in the Panama Canal Zone in 1936, not a state but considered by treaty to be sovereign US territory.

Perhaps because of sensitivity to the issue, McCain brought it up with regard to Texas state senator Ted Cruz early in the primary campaign season of 2016. Cruz was born in Calgary, Canada, although his mother was a US citizen, making him "natural born" under the terms of article II. Cruz's father was Cuban. Cruz maintained dual citizenship with Canada and the US until he renounced the former in 2014. He became the first Republican to declare his presidential candidacy in on March 23, 2015. Trump began making the point about questionable citizenship with Cruz in January 2016 in an interview with the *Washington Post*. Cruz initially responded with a tweet containing a link to the "Fonzie jumps the shark" episode of the TV show *Happy Days*, suggesting Trump's campaign resembled a TV show gone bad.

That description also might apply to the event that may have finalized Trump's presidential ambitions: the White House

Correspondents dinner of April 2011. Barack Obama's remarks at the dinner included a lampoon of Trump's association with birtherism and his then potential but unlikely bid for the presidency. Trump greeted Obama's remarks initially with a good-humored expression but that famously transformed into a deadly grimace as he sat in that audience. The transformation of what had been Donald Trump's flirtation with presidential politics into actual animus toward Obama and a will to power had been televised.

Trump picked up birtherism in part from Hillary Clinton campaigners who in 2008 circulated e-mails asserting a Kenyan birthplace for Obama. This became enhanced for Trump by Joseph Farah, founder of the rightist web site *WorldNetDaily*. Although Trump would claim that he sent lawyers to Hawaii to investigate the birther claim, it was Farah who led the publicity effort that eventually resulted in the release of two Barack Obama birth certificates: the computer-generated, notarized certificate of live birth released in 2008; and the long-form, released in 2011, the Hawaii Department of Health's certified original. Neither document fully satisfied critics. As late as January 2017 Joseph Farah continued to argue that more could be made of the birther eligibility story. One satisfied critic, though: Donald Trump. At the end of a press conference, he stated clearly, albeit a press conference to announce a new hotel on Pennsylvania Avenue that "President Barack Obama was born in the United States."

**TRUMPOCALYPSE REVELATIONS:
A CALENDAR OF TRUMP ADMINISTRATION HIGHLIGHTS**

February 2017
2/2
Attends the return of first military casualty of the Trump administration, a Navy SEAL killed in Yemen

**2/3**

Orders review of federal requirement for financial managers to act in the best interest of their clients

Eases regulations of the 2010 Dodd-Frank Wall Street Reform and Consumer Protection Act, instituted in response to economic recession

**2/9**

Prioritizes prosecution of foreign-based drug and human trafficking

Creates new federal task force on crime

Orders review of existing laws protecting police

**2/10 & 2/13**

Meets with foreign dignitaries from Japan and Canada

**2/14**

Signs first bill, ending Dodd-Frank transparency rule

National Security Adviser Michael Flynn resigns over secret contacts with Russia. The situation had been brought to Trump's attention by acting attorney general Sally Yates, who shortly thereafter was fired, ostensibly over the immigration ban issue.

**2/16**

At a press conference, referring to the leaks that led to the Flynn resignation, Trump declares: "The leaks are real. The leaks are absolutely real. The news is fake."

**2/17**

Trump's pick to replace Flynn, retired vice admiral Robert Harwood, declines the job

2/21

Chooses Lieutenant General H. R. McMaster for NSA vacancy

Demonstrators around the country observe "Not My President Day" protests

2/23

Tells reporters of his plan to expand the US nuclear arsenal

2/24

Speaks at Conservative Political Action Conference (CPAC)

2/25

Announces he will not attend the White House Correspondents Association Dinner; his attendance at a previous such event and rage over the ridicule he received there may have contributed to his decision to run for president.

White House Press Secretary Sean Spicer recently said members of the administration did not feel they needed to show up and "fake it," pretending to enjoy being roasted by the press. Also, given the administration's adversarial relationship with the press, many of the high-profile sponsors of the prestigious pre- and after-parties had previously announced that they would not be throwing their shindigs. Among them: Vanity Fair and Bloomberg; The New Yorker; Time/People; The Hill; Google; and Rock the Vote.

2/26

Trump's pick for Secretary of Navy withdraws

2/28

Delivers first speech to Congress, soft-pedaling his earlier positions

# Chapter 4
# 9/11 and Islamofascism

"What's the police and firemen down to seven eleven, down to
the World Trade Center right after it came down…"
—Donald Trump, *Wall Street Journal*, 4/19/16

Donald Trump gave this analysis of 9/11 to an interviewer for
WWOR-TV shortly after the events of that day:

> There was an architectural defect. You know the
> World Trade Center was always known as a very, very
> strong building. Don't forget that it took a big bomb in the
> basement. Now the basement is the most vulnerable place
> because that's your foundation. And it withstood that. And
> I got to see that area about three or four days after it took
> place because one of my structural engineers actually took
> me for a tour because he did the building. And I said I can't
> believe it. The building was standing solid and half of the
> columns were blown out. So this was an unbelievably
> powerful building.
>
> If you know anything about structure, it was one of the
> buildings that was built from the outside. The steel—the
> reason the World Trade Center had such narrow windows
> is that in between all the windows you have the steel on
> the outside. So you had the steel on the outside of the
> building. That's why when I first looked—and you had
> big, heavy I beams—when I first looked at it I couldn't
> believe it because there was a hole in the steel. This is
> steel that—you remember the width of the windows in
> the World Trade Center—if you were ever up there you
> remember they were quite narrow and in between was this

heavy steel.

How could a plane, even a plane, even a 767 or 747 or whatever it might have been, how could it possibly go through this steel? I happen to think they had not only a plane but that they had bombs that exploded almost simultaneously. I just can't imagine anything being able to go through that wall.

Most buildings are built where the steel is on the inside around the elevator shaft. This one was built from the outside, which was the strongest structure you can have. And it was almost like a can of soup…

I think there was a plane with more than just fuel. Obviously, they were very big planes and they were going very rapidly. I was watching where the planes seemed to be not only going fast but seemed to be coming down into the building. So it was getting speed from going downhill so to speak. It just seemed to me to do that kind of destruction it's even more than a big plane. You're talking about taking out steel, the heaviest caliber steel that was used on a building. These buildings were rock solid. You know, it's an amazing thing.

This country is different today and it's going to be different than it ever was for many years to come.

As the Trump campaign and presidency proceeded, these observations, versions of which provided the basis for the 9/11 Truth movement, became the least of the controversies regarding Donald Trump and 9/11, most famously, his claim that thousands of Muslims in New Jersey cheered in the streets after the buildings fell.

At one political rally Trump remarked, "I watched when the World Trade Center came tumbling down. And I watched in Jersey City, NJ, where thousands and thousands of people were cheering as that building was coming down. Thousands of people were cheering." He followed this up with a remark to the press: "It was on television. I saw it," Trump said. "It was well covered at the time...Now, I know they don't like to talk about it, but it was well covered at the time. There were people over in New Jersey that were watching it, a heavy Arab population that were cheering as the buildings came down. Not good." His description became a major example for his critics of Trump conflating reality with a television spectacle he only half-remembered. Mainstream media outlets pointed out that such celebrations did take place in Palestinian territories but after exhaustive computer searches could find only a single, unfounded story by the Associated Press on September 17, 2001 concerning rooftop celebrations by Muslims in New Jersey. On the following day *The Washington Post* ran an unsourced story reporting that "law enforcement authorities detained and questioned a number of people who were allegedly seen celebrating the attacks and holding tailgate-style parties on rooftops while they watched the devastation on the other side of the river." A similar report appeared in the *New York Post.*

Although the claim had other bits of corroboration—including comments by New York mayor Rudy Giuliani, radio and witness reports—Trump's description of the half-remembered TV report became the go-to example by his critics of an Islamophobic prejudice. That had its full measure of expression when Trump as president enacted a travel ban, later blocked in federal court, against a number of Muslim dominated states, including Syria, Iran, Sudan, Libya, Somalia, Yemen and Iraq, and also suspended the US refugee acceptance program.

Notably missing from the Islamic countries on the list: Saudi Arabia, the United Arab Emirates, Egypt, Lebanon, Turkey, and Indonesia. The hijackers in the 9/11 attacks included nineteen al-Qaeda operatives. Fifteen of those came from Saudi Arabia. The rest came from the UAE, Egypt, and Lebanon. One declassified government report, called "The 28 Pages," detailed how the Saudis funded Muslim radicals through charities and mosques at the time of 9/11. Trump had made a campaign issue of calling the enemy by its name, Islamofascism, but wound up supporting that ideology, especially in its transnational funding aspects.

Trump had in fact implicated Barack Obama in a conspiracy

with Saudi Arabia during the 2012 election. He maintained that the Saudis artificially suppressed the price of oil in order to make the American economy look good. He told one broadcaster, "If Obama got elected, you're going to see something with oil like you've never seen before, it will go through the roof. The favor will be repaid many times over." That never happened, of course, but the comment did reflect Trump's conspiratorial view of politics in the Middle East.

So critics took it as no surprise when Trump excluded his trading partners from the executive order banning travel to the US from major Islamic countries. Trump had no business ties with any of the countries on the banned list. He had development and licensing contracts with many of the rest. His attitude toward Saudi Arabia changed in August 2015 when, just after his declaration to run for US president, he registered eight hotel related companies there. Of the former Obama co-conspirators Trump said, "They buy apartments from me," he said. "They spend $40 million, $50 million. Am I supposed to dislike them? I like them very much."

## TRUMPOCALYPSE REVELATIONS
### A UFO ENCOUNTERS TRUMP

An unidentified flying object buzzed Donald Trump's helicopter as he flew over the Iowa State Fair during the 2016 campaign. A cameraman was present who later told *Daily Express,* "We were walking down the street to the fair. Donald Trump's helicopter was flying overhead so I got my phone out and snapped a picture." The photo seems to show a flying saucer but is blurry enough that the object could be construed as a bird or another helicopter. The reporter turned the image over to the Iowa Mutual UFO Network.

## TRUMPOCALYPSE REVELATIONS
## A CALENDAR OF TRUMP ADMINISTRATION
## HIGHLIGHTS

March 2017
3/3
His most recent trip to the Mar-a-Lago resort in Palm Beach, Florida brings the amount of time spent there to one-fourth the amount of time Trump has spent as president

3/4
Trump tweets: "Terrible! Just found out that Obama had my "wires tapped" in Trump Tower just before the victory. Nothing found. This is McCarthyism." Several tweets follow repeating the accusation.

3/6
Pro and anti Trump activists clash in Berkeley, CA

3/8
"A Day Without Women" general strike observed in protest of Trump

3/9
Cancels multiple press events to avoid discussing tweets

3/11
Trump fires Preet Bharara, US Attorney for the Southern District of New York known as a crusader against bank and hedge fund corruption, who refused to resign

3/15
"Ides of Trump" postcard campaign bombards Trump with messages of opposition

3/15
Federal judge in Hawaii stops Trump's revised travel ban

3/15
House Intelligence committee announces that it has found no evidence that Obama wiretapped Trump or otherwise had Trump under surveillance

3/20
FBI director James Comey tells the House committee that he has no information "that supports those tweets."

3/21
Devin Nunes, head of the House Intelligence Committee investigating Trump's ties to Russia, switches cars after taking a phone call and makes an unscheduled visit to the White House. There he receives information about incidental collection of intelligence on the Trump administration legally gathered during sanctioned investigations. He later briefs the White House on the information he received from the White House, but does not brief the Intelligence Committee.

3/24
Nunes cancels planned open Intelligence Committee hearing. (Nunes steps down from leadership of the Intelligence Committee on April 6.)

3/27
Trump creates new Office of American Innovation and puts son-in-law Jared Kusher in charge of it

# Chapter 5

# Clinton Conspiracies

"I agree with everything she said."
—Donald Trump, presidential debate

During and before the course of his presidential campaign, Donald Trump leveled many conspiracy accusations against his Democratic opponent, Hillary Clinton. Perhaps most prominent on the list had to do with the September 11, 2012 attacks on the US diplomatic compound in Benghazi, Libya that resulted in the murders of J. Christopher Stevens, American ambassador to Libya, and Foreign Service information officer Sean Smith. Hillary Clinton's e-mail from this time, when she served as US Secretary of State, became a central focus for many of her political and congressional critics, and the subject of hearings by a congressional select committee.

The controversy devolved into a question of Clinton's discretion in using a private e-mail server for official communications. Clinton admitted to that charge and also to deleting a large number of e-mails from the period, which led to significant political fallout and plenty of fodder for Donald Trump's campaign. When charges surfaced that Russians had hacked the computer servers of the Democratic National Committee, Trump declared at a news conference: "Russia, if you're listening, I hope you're able to find the 30,000 e-mails that are missing." Thus began the pivot away from the Clinton e-mail controversy to the issues surrounding Trump's relationship to Russia.

An assassination lurked underneath that otherwise typical political folderol. DNC staff member Seth Rich was shot and killed a short distance from his home in Bloomingdale, a DC neighborhood. Rich had been shot in the back. Police suspected robbery but Rich's girlfriend told the press "There had been a struggle. His hands were bruised, his knees are bruised, his face is bruised, and yet he had two shots to his back, and yet they never took anything… They didn't finish robbing him, they just took his life."

The crime remains unsolved, but as suspicions began to accrue about Donald Trump's connections to Russia, researchers revisited Rich's murder for its parapolitical implications. *The Washington Post* reported that Russian hackers leaked thousands of e-mails and documents from the Democratic National Committee in an effort to aid Donald Trump's campaign. Trump's defenders declared this a red herring, that Rich had done the leaking on behalf of a wealthy backer of presidential candidate Bernie Sanders. Wikileaks founder Julian Assange implied that Rich leaked the documents to him and because of it Hillary Clinton had him murdered.

The controversy took an even more bizarre turn with the development of the Pizzagate theory. The wiki-leaked e-mails—specifically those of Hillary Clinton's presidential campaign chairman John Podesta—supposedly included coded nods to a pedophile ring operating out of pizza restaurants on behalf of high-ranking members of the DNC. The idea had its origins in rumors surrounding the infamous sexting scandal of congressman Anthony Weiner. The theory maintained that the New York police department discovered evidence on Weiner's laptop of a DNC-connected human trafficking ring with elements of satanic ritual abuse. Coded references to this supposedly could be found in the Podesta e-mails—the use of handkerchief signals figured prominently. Such rumors had long accompanied stories of a group called the Finders in DC. According to the theory, Podesta's brother Tony had some connection to the notorious disappearance in Portugal of a British girl named Madeleine McCann. Substantive evidence for any of this never materialized.

The rumors, however, convinced Edgar Maddison Welch. In December 2016 he brought an automatic weapon and a .38 caliber revolver from North Carolina to the Comet Ping Pong, the pizza place mentioned in the Podesta e-mails as being at the center of the Pizzagate stories. Having heard about Pizzagate on Alex Jones' InfoWars program, Welch fired shots into the Comet Ping Pong. He hit no one but later pled guilty to assault and gun charges. *Infowars'* Alex Jones later apologized for his role in circulating the Pizzagate rumors.

As much as partisans like to believe that conspiracy accusations arise only out of opposition political research, suspicions and accusations dogged the Clintons throughout their careers from a variety of sources. In an article I wrote that appeared in the *Washington Post* on January 16, 1995, I reviewed the then current discussions about parapolitcs under the Clinton administration. Entitled "Clinton Era Conspiracies! Was Gennifer Flowers on the Grassy Knoll? Probably Not But Here are Some Other Bizarre Theories for a New Political Age":

> As a teenager I heard John Kennedy's summons to citizenship. And then, as a student at Georgetown, I heard that call clarified by a professor named Carroll Quigley, who said to us that America was the greatest nation in history because our people have always believed two things: that tomorrow can be better than today, and that every one of us has a personal, moral responsibility to make it so.
>
> — from Bill Clinton's acceptance speech to the Democratic National Convention, 1992

To most of those who watched the Arkansas governor accept his party's nomination for the presidency, these words had no special resonance beyond their inspirational tone. But for the nationwide networks of researchers who probe the tangled webs of intrigue, the words marked the dawn of a new age of conspiracy theory, one that may do for the '90s what the JFK assassination and the Trilateral Commission did for eras past.

Carroll Quigley, the Georgetown University professor whose

51

memory was invoked by Clinton, had already been flagged by conspiracy theorists as one of their own, a theoretician of the one-world secret cabal. A respected academician, Quigley authored a 1966 book, *Tragedy and Hope: A History of the World in Our Time*, that has long been regarded by right-wingers (even cited in televangelist Pat Robertson's books) as a codex to the hidden ambitions of those generally well-regarded pillars of the foreign policy establishment, the Trilateral Commission and the Council on Foreign Relations. By invoking Quigley, Clinton had virtually telegraphed to the conspiratorial cognoscenti a signal to start massaging their databases.

Response to that signal was impressive. Conspiracy researchers found enough raw material to keep themselves busy well throughout the Clinton presidency and beyond.

No question, the conspiracy research community—a loose collegium of competing schools of conjecture, unbound by the normal constraints of academic or journalistic verification or disproof—needed the feast set before it by the Clinton administration. The 30th anniversary of JFK's death had passed; while the staid *Wall Street Journal* was characterizing JFK researchers as primitively malicious, no less a hip source than "Doonesbury" creator Garry Trudeau lambasted them in the funny pages. Ex-CIA chief George H.W. Bush had been ousted from the Oval Office; such Reagan offenses as the October Surprise seemed like ancient history. Something new was clearly indicated. Make what you want of it all, but following is a look at some of the main strands in Clinton-age conspiracy thinking.

## THE QUIGLEY CONNECTION

Before Carroll Quigley died in 1977 he had come to be viewed as almost a reverse barometer by highly paranoid elements of the conspiracy community such as the ultra-right John Birch Society—when Quigley said something was good, that was taken as a signal that it was bad. Both Quigley and the Birchers agreed the world was run by a secret cabal of Rockefellers, Rothschilds, Morgans and like-minded financiers. In "Tragedy and Hope,"

Quigley described the operations of the behind-the-scene players in international affairs. The book's thesis, however, was not critical of these arrangements. Rather, Quigley viewed it as a "benevolent conspiracy," in the words of Jonathan Vankin, author of *Conspiracies, Cover Ups and Crimes* (published by Paragon House, which is owned by the Rev. Sun Myung Moon's Unification Church). The Birchers were enraged by what they viewed as the confession of an insider, a player himself in the globe's power structure. They began listing Quigley's book regularly in the footnotes of their books as proof of the monied interests behind their bugaboos, groups like the Trilateralists. That Clinton referred to the late professor on a regular basis throughout the campaign and virtually enshrined him at the Democratic National Convention caused some to laud Quigley's work as the rhetorical foundation of the new administration's political philosophy. In the conspiracy realm, it caused others to review Quigley's research.

Writer Jim Martin, whose definitive biography on Wilhelm Reich, *Wilhelm Reich and the Cold War* includes much on Quigley, points out that Quigley's main research involved the Rhodes-Milner Group. This informal discussion group of financiers, founded by 19th century British industrialist Cecil Rhodes, had real connections to both the Morgans and the Rothschilds. Martin also points out that Cecil Rhodes was one of the world's wealthiest men, that he had a country named after him (Rhodesia), that his will founded and funded the Rhodes scholarships and that Bill Clinton is a Rhodes scholar. "The function of the Rhodes scholarships," explains Martin, "was to identify future leaders, instill them with common values at Oxford and send them back to their native colonies where they could spread these acquired traits."

Researcher Len Bracken explores the disparity between Clinton's evocation of Quigley as an idealist and Quigley's own hard-nosed views in an issue of *Steamshovel Press*. In a study of speeches by Quigley made 10 years after Clinton left Georgetown, Bracken finds this assessment of the American state in one of Quigley's last speeches: "Today everything is a bureaucratic structure, and brainwashed people who are not personalities are trained to fit into this bureaucratic structure and say it is a great life—although I would assume that many on their death beds must feel otherwise. The process of copping out will take a long time…" This is a far cry from the Carroll Quigley who exhorted Bill Clinton to make each tomorrow better than today.

## THE MENA MESS

Less intellectual entanglements between the Clintons and the conspiracy netherworld have occupied the attention of researchers at least since April 1992. In that month, a decidedly non-intellectual source, Geraldo Rivera's old *Now It Can Be Told* infotainment/tabloid, ran two stories—based in part on earlier stories by Alexander Cockburn in *The Nation*—on drug smuggling, money laundering and the possible movement of Nicaraguan contras in and out of an airstrip in the small Arkansas town of Mena. The case has since been expanded upon in the *Village Voice*; Paul Krassner has brought it to the attention of the readers of his satirical newsletter, *The Realist*, and it took up an entire chapter of John Bainerman's book *The Crimes of a President*, which offers itself as an expose of Bush administration abuses.

The alleged cover-up in Mena promised to be the weak link in a chain that entangled Clinton not only with Bush but also with Oliver North's secret network of operatives and under-the-counter involvement in the Contra War.

The Mena story begins with a major drug trafficker named Barry Seal who apparently began smuggling drugs through the airstrip in 1982. The operation continued past Seal's 1984 drug conviction in Miami. As Seal was working deals with the Drug Enforcement Administration (DEA) and North's network, trading undercover work against the Sandinistas for leniency, according to Bainerman, a second wave of mysterious businesses descended upon the Intermountain Regional Airport at Mena. These businesses described themselves variously as aircraft and parts-delivery services, but stories of drug traffic continued. In 1989, new allegations were made by a former criminal investigator for the U.S. military, Gene Wheaton, that the airfield was also used for commando training. The Arkansas state police investigated and reported to the U.S. attorney, but the expected indictments were never returned, leading to the suspicion that the Reagan administration could add one more small cover-up to its tally.

Clinton does not enter the story until April 1992, when a pair of students at the University of Arkansas, Mark Swaney and Tom Brown, appealed directly to their then-governor to investigate. The appeal, and another call for financial assistance for a state grand jury investigation from Arkansas' deputy prosecuting attorney, met a stone wall. When Arkansas Rep. Bill Alexander met with Clinton, according to Bainerman, he was told that a scant $25,000 in state money had been set aside to investigate Mena, but even that was never delivered. The prosecuting attorney in Mena's Polk County at the time said he never received the offer from the governor's office.

The IRS began an investigation of Seal's operation in Mena after Seal was murdered in Baton Rouge by Colombian drug traffickers in 1986. But according to Bill Duncan, a former IRS investigator, the investigators were warned off, causing Duncan to quit and testify before a House committee about all he had learned of money laundering, covert operations and drug smuggling in Mena.

The claim that Clinton was remiss in not investigating Mena was first made publicly by Larry Nichols in a defamation suit against the governor. Clinton had hired Nichols as marketing director for the Arkansas Development Finance Authority but fired him when his alleged contacts with the contras became apparent, citing the charge that Nichols had made unauthorized phone calls to Central America as reason for the firing. In Nichols's subsequent lawsuit contesting that charge, he also first publicized the claims of Gennifer Flowers to have had an affair with Bill Clinton.

Another court case, that of Terry Reed, described by Bainerman as a CIA contract operative, also added to the Mena story. In 1988 Reed was charged with postal fraud for receiving insurance money on a false claim. Reed claimed that his airplane had been stolen as part of a project called "Private Donation," wherein "donations" to the contra cause were filed as lost or stolen with insurance companies and then reimbursed. According to Reed, he had no awareness of "Project Donation" at the time of his plane's disappearance and so reported it as a legitimate loss. The plane reappeared after Reed learned of the donation project and warned his contacts in the North network that he would have no part of it.

The person who first reported the discovery of what turned out to be Reed's plane to the National Crime Information Center was Raymond L. (Buddy) Young, then working for Bill Clinton as security chief and later chosen by Clinton to head the Dallas regional office of the Federal Emergency Management Agency. Federal Judge Frank Theis later said that Young and an associate "acted with reckless disregard for the truth" in their version of how they came to realize the plane was not stolen, and charges against Reed were dropped.

### WACO WEIRDNESS

At a candlelight vigil held in Dealey Plaza by Citizens for the Truth About the Kennedy Assassination on its 30th anniversary, a suggestion that President Clinton might join in the event was met with a lukewarm smattering of applause. Had not the Clinton administration emasculated the Assassination Materials Review Act of 1992 by delaying its nominations to the review board? Clinton did not show and later made a statement that he believed that Lee Harvey Oswald acted alone.

For those who attended the Assassination Symposium on Kennedy (ASK) for which the vigil was organized, it was not the only sign that Clinton's claims to affinity with JFK were bogus. Jack White, who has done an enormous amount of work analyzing a large inventory of Oswald photographs, flashed a slide before his ASK presentation. It showed a tank backing away from the destruction at the Branch Davidian compound with flame ostensibly spewing from its cannon. "The coverups continue!" exclaimed White.

The scene came from a videotape entitled "Waco: The Big Lie" circulated by the America Justice Federation, which is headed by Linda Thompson, who filed a petition during the Waco siege to represent David Koresh and his followers. The tape is said to contain a detailed view of the bungled BATF raid taken by Ken Engleman, contributor to the book, *Secret and Suppressed*. The tape is said to be from an unedited satellite feed from a video transmission by a foreign correspondent covering the raid. Other viewers say the alleged flames coming from the tank are just debris from the conflagration falling in front of the tank as it backs out after destroying a wall of the compound. What has not been challenged, however, is Thompson's assertion that three of the murdered agents had been among Clinton's many bodyguards during the presidential campaign.

Thompson also claims the tape shows that the alleged former bodyguards were actually killed by a fourth BATF agent, either deliberately or with reckless application of the "spray and pray" method of gunfire used after the three had entered a rooftop window.

## THE BODY COUNT

Dave Emory does a syndicated radio program originating in California's Santa Clara Valley called "One Step Beyond" in which he reads into the public record various kinds of research material he has collected from newspapers, magazines and books, puts the material into a context by linking similar and connected stories and offers tapes to listeners for review. Through this method, Emory has reached an interesting conclusion about the mortality rate in the Clinton campaign and administration: It exceeds what would ordinarily be expected from a study of the laws of statistical probability.

In addition to the suicide of White House assistant counsel Vince Foster, Emory notes that two important Clinton campaign aides died during the campaign. Also, the woman who had been doing sign language interpretation of Clinton's speeches for the hearing-impaired and was scheduled to do the same at the inauguration died unexpectedly before Clinton took the oath, at age 36. Presumably, the statistical wave now includes the bodyguard deaths at Waco. Emory offers a reminder that natural deaths and accidents can be easily faked with the resources available to the intelligence community. Although he makes no direct charges in this regard, he does place the statistical anomaly in a category familiar to his listeners: food for thought and grounds for further research.

## INMAN THE SPACEMAN

Extraterrestrial theories are frequently thrown into the conspiracy milieu as comic relief, although conspiracists note that flying saucer rumors are often injected into situations where real leaks of government secrets occur in order to deprive those situations of any credibility. But the disinformation theory has yet to be applied to Clinton's nominee for Secretary of Defense, retired admiral Bobby Ray Inman, since the only known improprieties of his past involve tax discrepancies apparently shared by many Clinton nominees (save for the suggestion in Jim Hougan's 1984 book, *Secret Agenda*, that Inman might have been Deep Throat of Watergate fame). Inman figures prominently in at least one UFO researcher's tale, however.

*Alien Contact* is a follow-up to author Timothy Good's *Above Top Secret*, a book well-received among ufologists for its documentation of international government interest in UFOs. In it, he describes the efforts of a retired NASA engineer named Robert Oeschler to contact Inman and discuss military knowledge of extraterrestrial craft because of Inman's extensive background with technology-related government projects. Oeschler approached Inman after a speech and handed him a note requesting that the admiral help get him in closer contact with MJ12, alleged in UFO lore to be a secret government liaison group with space aliens. Inman, according to Oeschler, said okay.

More than a year later, Oeschler, who occupies some of his retirement with being assistant state director for the Mutual UFO Network in Maryland, says he phoned Inman to discuss MJ12 and perhaps gain some access to government data on extraterrestrial craft. Inman, says Oeschler, demurred that he had retired from intelligence work and was seven years out of date on any such information.

Oeschler continued, "Do you anticipate that any of the recovered [extraterrestrial] vehicles would ever become available for technological research—outside military circles?" according to Good, who says he was present during the phone conversation. "Ten years ago the answer would have been no," Inman is said to have replied. "Whether as time has evolved they are beginning to become more open about it, there's a possibility." Good also says that while Inman now denies any knowledge of UFOs, he admitted in a signed letter to Good that this was the topic of his phone conversation with Oeschler.

### THE FOSTER DEATH

The suicide of Vincent Foster in July of 1993 left a conspiratorial quagmire. The circumstances of the death, a wound inflicted by an antique gun, were quickly overshadowed by questions of motive. Was, some asked, Foster driven to such an extreme by an aspect of his involvement with the Rose Law Firm in Little Rock in which Hillary Clinton was a partner? Was there a connection with the Whitewater Development Corp. real estate partnership whose files were, it was subsequently revealed, removed from Foster's office shortly after his death? The conspiracy mill attached the scandal to international murder plots and long-standing connections between Clinton, George Bush and the Atlanta branch of the Italian state bank, Banca Nazionale del Lavaro (BNL).

Researcher Sherman Skolnick, who has prominent in conspiratorial circles since Watergate, insisted Foster died trying to prevent a CIA-aided assassination of Saddam Hussein in July 1993. Such a plot, but not a supposed Foster connection, was later reported upon in the *London Sunday Times*. Foster did not attempt to do this out of love for Saddam or even to make tomorrow better than today, according to Skolnick's scenario. He did it to prevent Saddam's half-brother from releasing bank records revealing Clinton and Bush involvement with BNL.

An official of the Atlanta branch of BNL, Christopher Drogoul, was sentenced for laundering money used in Saddam's buildup before the first Gulf War. But the bank was also fingered as a presence in the JFK assassination in a 23-year-old document that makes a series of extraordinary claims—so extraordinary that it is controversial even in conspiracy circles. Known as the Torbitt Document, it claimed in 1970 that BNL had financed training of the hit team used against Kennedy. A connection had been made between the labyrinth of the JFK assassination and the burgeoning Clinton conspiracies.

In the end, Skolnick is not clear on what kept Foster from making the fateful appointment that was to block the plot, or how the plot failed anyway. He also asserts, however, that former FBI director William Sessions was removed for something related to the Clinton-Bush-BNL connection and that Foster was actually a victim of an assassination team from Germany.

In addition to supplying a snapshot of the conspiracy research community of the time, the article identified parapolitical situations that continued to warrant debate until supplanted by the new batch Trump introduced in the 2016 campaign, following eight years of the Obama administration and Hillary Clinton's important role in it. Back in 1997, the Clinton White House acknowledged the burgeoning interest in parapolitcal study—"conspiracy theories" had been Internet fodder for a number of years by then—and sought to develop its own conspiracy theory to deal with it. It created a 322-page report entitled "Communication Stream of Conspiracy Commerce," featuring the *Washington Post* article prominently. The report made headlines when details of its contents emerged in the Washington newspapers.

The report suggested that right-wing ideologues would suggest rumors that got picked up by the British press and then got transformed into hard news to be reported in the mainstream American press, a media food chain without which, according to the report, nothing bad ever would have been written about the Clinton administration. Such a view, according to the Post, "has long been expressed by Clinton strategist James Carville and other Clinton advisers" but the report "lays down the suspicion laden theories in cold-print, under the imprimatur of the White House."

The sources quoted in my original *Washington Post* article, of course, were all American. The only theory disproven was that of the White House special report, the "conspiracy commerce" stream. In the national press, Hillary Clinton's characterization of this as a "vast-right-wing conspiracy" became a bit of a lampoon, a trend that magnified under the Trump campaign of 2016. Trump rode that misunderstanding—a culture of ridicule that blossomed into the stuff of late night TV comedy and blindsided TV news channels that underestimated Trump's political clout—to a White House victory.

## TRUMPOCALYPSE REVELATIONS
### WIKIFIED UFOLOGY

The many revelations of the wiki-leaked e-mails of Hillary Clinton's campaign chairman John Podesta included many of his online communications with the likes of Edgar Mitchell and other ufologists. This gave Clinton cred with that crowd, which as ever hoped for the declassification of government files on UFOs, Area 51 and recovered alien technology. One MUFON director told the press, "There have been people within the community working with Podesta and the Clintons on the subject. Just having the conversation is very positive to realize the subject is real, and these intelligences, wherever they're from, visit us from time to time."

Podesta's communication with Terri Mansfield, an aide to the late Edgar Mitchell, the sixth man to walk on the moon, included this statement from Mansfield, "We work with specific ETI [extraterrestrial intelligence] from a contiguous universe. They are nonviolent and in complete obedience to God. Our ETI's connection to zero point energy is obvious in that their purpose is to guide Edgar's international Quantrek science team to apply their zero point energy research for humanity, to move away from the use of fossil fuels which are so deleterious to our fragile planet." Trump, of course, supported fracking and other means to continue development of fossil fuels.

Podesta previously had been known as a UFO enthusiast. In 2002, according to Leslie Kean, author of *UFOs: Generals, Pilots and Government Officials Go on the Record* (which had a foreword by Podesta) Podesta began publicly supporting a Freedom of Information Act lawsuit over government records concerning the 1965 Kecksburg, Pennsylvania UFO incident. The lawsuit led to the release of some documents but nothing on Kecksburg. Podesta had also spoken at a 2002 National Press Club event to encourage the release of government files on flying saucers. John Podesta began as deputy chief of staff for Bill Clinton in 1997.

# Chapter 6

# Assasinologist

"Lyndon Johnson once told an aide to characterize a political enemy as a 'swinophiliac.' When asked what that was, Johnson responded, "I don't know, but at least we can get him to deny it."
—Robert Anton Wilson

Donald Trump entered into the world of JFK assassination studies big league during the 2016 campaign when on the day following his acceptance of the Republican nomination he tweeted the idea that the father of his primary opponent Ted Cruz was photographed with Lee Harvey Oswald handing out Fair Play for Cuba leaflets in New Orleans in August 1963. He later told a TV show that Cruz's father, Rafael, "was with Lee Harvey Oswald prior to Oswald's being, you know, shot! I mean, the whole thing is ridiculous … And nobody even brings it up. I mean, they don't even talk about that, that was reported and nobody talks about it. But I think it's horrible, I think it's absolutely horrible, that a man can go and do that, what he's saying there. I mean what was he doing with Lee Harvey Oswald, shortly before the death—before the shooting? It's horrible."

Critics quickly pointed out that Trump's only source for the defamatory accusation was the well-known and ill-reputed tabloid, the *National Enquirer*. It ran the report on April 20, 2016, citing as proof only the opinion of a man, Mitch Goldstone, identified as a photograph expert who declared that a photo from the period had "more similarity than dissimilarity" with Rafael Cruz's passport photograph. Goldstone later told the press that he never

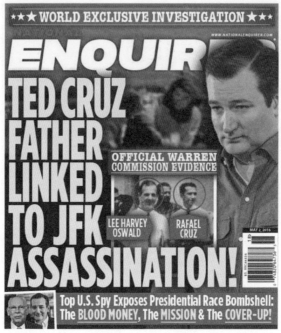

The *National Enquirer* reports the JFK assassination link to Trump's political opponent during the primary, Ted Cruz.

made the unqualified assertion but simply pointed out the strong similarity of the images. He called Trump's assertion about it "stupid."

That the story appeared in the *National Enquirer*, widely decried for its sensationalism, became *a priori* evidence of Donald Trump's lack of credibility if not sanity. Trump, of course, saw it differently. He told one reporter, "All I did is point out the fact that on the cover of the *National Enquirer* there's a picture of him [Rafael Cruz] and crazy Lee Harvey Oswald having breakfast. I had nothing to do with it. This was a magazine that frankly in many respects should be very respected. They got OJ. They got Edwards. They got this. I mean if that was the *New York Times*, they would have gotten Pulitzer prizes for their reporting." Criticism of the *New York Times* and other "mainstream media" became an important issue in the early months of Trump's presidency but the critique never extended to the *Enquirer.*

The short version of that story began and ended in the last bitter

Lee Harvey Oswald handing out pro-Castro leaflets.

battles of that election campaign. The Cruz camp and Rafael Cruz himself denied the accusation. But the fact that a man identified as Rafael Cruz in the photograph had never been identified by any official investigation of the assassination left a door open for speculation by more than that *National Enquirer*'s photo expert. In April 2016 researcher Wayne Madsen noted that "based on the presence of the elder Cruz, an anti-Castro activist, in Dallas and New Orleans before the November 22, 1963, assassination of President John F. Kennedy, there is a strong reason to believe that Cruz was associated with the Central Intelligence Agency's anti-Castro operations." He continues, "Furthermore, a Cuban hired by alleged JFK assassin Lee Harvey Oswald and who bears a striking resemblance to Cruz is seen in an iconic photograph of Oswald and a group of Cubans Oswald hired who were distributing "Hands off

Oswald and "Rafael Cruz" handing out pro-Castro leaflets.

Cuba!" pamphlets in New Orleans in the summer of 1963. The photo of Oswald and other Cubans he hired for the Fair Play for Cuba Committee was taken outside the International Trade Mart in New Orleans on August 16, 1963."

It was, of course, just conspiratorial speculation but it was not quite the insinuation that it appeared. Many students of the JFK assassination believe those "pro-Castro" demonstrators in 1963 New Orleans, including Oswald and possibly Cruz, are actually anti-Castro operatives working for a spy cell run by Guy Bannister, an FBI figure whose history goes back to the Maury Island UFO incident of 1947. Their purpose was to infiltrate and collect intelligence on New Orleans' pro-Castro population. Another possible purpose: set up Lee Oswald as a pro-Castro sympathizer to later frame him for JFK's murder. In any event, that would make Rafael Cruz, or whoever that person with Oswald was, another agent, heroically performing a patriotic and dangerous task. The distinction was lost on Donald Trump and his critics.

The Trump campaign had one other link to the JFK lore: the

Cruz's father would have been working for a fake pro-Castro intelligence operation with Oswald. The New Orleans counterintelligence operation was run by Guy Bannister, also an operative in the 1947 Maury Island UFO case.

weird predictive power of the television spectacle. An example of this phenomenon occurred in March of 2001 when a conspiracy television show called *The Lone Gunmen* had as its plot planes crashing into the World Trade Towers in New York—a scenario that predicted the events of the following September. Similarly, Donald Trump's presidency was predicted by the cartoon *The Simpsons* in the year 2000 when one of its characters, Lisa Simpson, becomes president in a futuristic scenario after President Trump brings the country to economic ruin. Online, this morphed into a rumor that the cartoon had visually predicted Trump's famed elevator ride after filing for the office. Proof of this actually turned out to be only a *Simpsons* parody of the event.

Documents for Rafael Cruz, Ted Cruz's Cuban-born father.

## TRUMPOCALYPSE REVELATIONS
### ON THE ROAD WITH TRUMP: THE PREDICTIVE SPECTACLE

The *Simpsons'* predicting Trump provides perhaps a trivial example of the predictive power of conspiracy spectacle but also one that offers a link between two television-friendly presidents. The strange TV predictors of the JFK assassination were far less trivial.

An episode of the old *Route 66* show called "Aren't You Surprised To See Me?" opened in Dallas/Fort Worth with the villain making a connection at Love Field, the airport into which JFK flew on the day he was killed more than a year later. The protagonists of the show, TV's version of Jack Kerouac and Neal Cassady driving "on the road" in a '62 Corvette, get jobs at the Trade Mart, where JFK planned to give a speech the day he died. At one point in the episode someone talking on the phone references Earle Cabell, the Dallas mayor whose brother Charles was fired by JFK as deputy director of the CIA because of the Bay of Pigs failure.

*Route 66* is known for having captured in its backgrounds the authentic American cultural landscape before it became homogenized into shopping malls. So here viewers find a straight look at the Dallas environs from the time of the assassination. The plot involved one of the guys (George Maharis, playing the Cassady figure but looking and talking a lot more like Kerouac) being kidnapped by a killer ready to dose the entire town with a deadly biotoxin. The killer is a religious fanatic who soliloquizes about absolute morality while Maharis/Cassady talks moral relativism. So it gives a picture of the kind of values debate happening on mainstream television at the time as well.

The eerie associations do not stop at that point on *Route 66*, however. In a separate episode, "Love Is a Skinny Kid," filmed in Lewisville, Texas at the same time as the one in Dallas, Tuesday Weld plays a character called Miriam Moore, a name that obviously looks like Marilyn Monroe sideways. Her character wears a mask that she refues to take off, upsetting the townfolk. The opening shot shows Maharis and Milner driving past a highway sign indicating the upcoming towns: Dallas, Waco (in Texas weirdland alright) and the town where the action takes place, Kilkenny, a word that looks like "Kill Kennedy" sideways.

The episode was filmed in 1962, again, one year before the assassination. Of the three towns, Kilkenny stands out as the only one that's totally fictional, created for the episode. A Kilkenny exists in Ireland and there's a street called Kilkenny in Texas, but not a town. News clippings appear online discussing how the *Route 66* TV production crew gave the town of Lewisville a makeover to turn it into the fictional Kilkenny.

Tuesday Weld steps off the bus into Kilkenny wearing what looks like a Guy Fawkes mask that she refuses to remove. She walks to her mother's house and burns a doll at the stake in front of it. As the plot unfolds, the viewer discovers that as a young girl Weld's character had a friend tie her to a tree and then tried to set fire to herself. For this she was institutionalized and banished from the town. Druid occultism? She explains to one of her former schoolteachers that her behavior was a product of a school system that didn't attend to the special needs of the children "bored with two plus two."

The JFK links all appear in the two episodes as just predictive coincidences. Dialogue in the Weld episode also includes a reference to *V for Vendetta*, referring to Weld's need to spook the townfolk with the mask. The strange mask looks a lot like the one that Alan Moore's character wears in his famous *V for Vendetta* graphic novel, published in 1982.

Another weird JFK-*Route 66* fact: the network canceled

the episode from a week after the assassination, November 29, 1963, and that one never aired during the show's original run. It had as its plot the bizarre coincidence of the character played by Martin Milner encountering a political assassin, his physical twin, also played by Milner. JFK students recall the multiple Oswald twins seen around Dallas the week before the intended original broadcast. The title of the episode: "To Kill a King."

At one point Jack Kerouac planned to sue the producers of *Route 66* for ripping off his novel. At the time, he said of the show that he abhorred its violence.

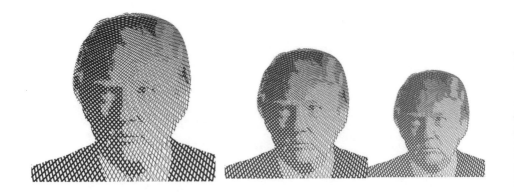

# Chapter 7

# The Parapolitics of Russia

"There are a lot of killers. We've got a lot of killers.
What do you think? Our country's so innocent?"
—Donald Trump to Bill O'Reilly

A week before Trump's inauguration, reports emerged accusing Donald Trump of covert connections to the Russian government. The file on this originated with a man named Christopher Steele, a former MI6 operative who disappeared of his own accord after releasing it. Although it has yet to be determined whether it is the most or the least scandalous part of its content, the dossier contained the uncomfortable detail that Trump had been set up with prostitutes and was videotaped participating in a "golden shower"—sexual activity involving urination. Russians refer to a file of such compromising information, useful for blackmail, as *kompromat.* Previously in the US, a videotape from the television show *Access Hollywood* surfaced with Trump commenting about women, "when you're a star they let you do it, you can do anything... grab them by the pussy."

This and a laundry list of financial improprieties with Russians ostensibly made Trump susceptible to blackmail. Steele's file also contained indications that Trump's presidential campaign allied with these Russian entities to enhance its chances of winning the election. A rumored "golden showers" video provided the stick and political favors provided the carrot in combination to make Donald Trump a useful idiot successfully

British MI6 agent Christopher Steele

manipulated into the top office of the US government. Moreover, the material also indicated that the Russians had been cultivating Trump for at least five years prior to his presidential run.

Steele's file found its way into the hands of American intelligence services, which after some deliberation in turn handed it over to the Obama White House and the Trump campaign. Obama made little issue of it until after the vote in order to limit its impact on an already compromised election result. It has, however, colored Trump's early tenure in the office and remains the subject of further and expanding government investigation. Steele's entire dossier is included in this book as an appendix.

As that scandal continues to bubble to the surface, it becomes more important to understand the less secret facts of parapolitics in Russia. Crucial to this is some review of the assassinations and attempted assassinations that have characterized modern Russian politics. In some ways, these killings have shaped the worldview of Russia just as the assassinations of the 60s political leaders shaped the worldview of American politics.

POLONIUM-210

The former Russian spy and political dissident Alexander Litvinenko dies after exposure to the rare radioactive poison Polonium-210. The name of the radioactive element Polonium-210 derives from the word Poland, the territory where its discoverer, Marie Curie, was born. In the late 1880s, Poland had no independence from Russia, a fact Madame Curie and her husband felt they could draw some public attention to by thus naming one of their other discoveries. Perhaps their efforts were successful: the territory gained its sovereignty after the First World War.

Polonium-210 is an extremely rare metal. It is highly radioactive in all its forms, releasing energetic alpha particles that cause the surrounding air to glow faintly and generating enough heat that it has been used in some spacecraft to prevent freezing of internal components. Its high radioactivity makes it very rare in nature, so any significant amount must be synthesized at great expense. As a result, it is very rarely available outside industrial or aeronautical processes. The alpha particles it produces cannot pass through skin, making it relatively harmless unless ingested, inhaled or otherwise absorbed into the body. However, once inside the body in even small amounts, it causes massive, acute radiation poisoning. Alpha particles released into the intestines and vital organs damage fragile cells, causing organ failure and death. The minimum lethal dose for an average human being is estimated to be about 50 nanograms, or billionths of a gram, although in practice—because radioactive decay takes place over time—an amount closer to one microgram, or millionth of a gram, may be required.

On November 23, 2006, 43 years and a day after the JFK assassination, former secret police agent Alexander Litvinenko died from polonium poisoning. Obviously not an accident, an understanding of this important political assassination takes a review of some recent Russian history.

The territory struggling for its sovereignty in the background of the Litvinenko assassination was Chechnya, north of the Caucasus Mountains and the Caspian Sea. The central event from which a list of suspicious deaths accrued happened at an apartment complex bombing on September 13, 1999 that killed or wounded over 300 Chechnyan citizens. It was the most recent in a series of bombing incidents that Vladimir Putin's government blamed on separatists and used as the pretext for a war to secure Russia's dominance of the province. Many in Russia saw this incident as a false flag operation masterminded by the Russian government to justify a military response.

Anna Politkovskaya

## ANNA POLITKOVSKAYA

Anna Politkovskaya enjoyed a reputation as one of the best-known journalists to decry the ongoing Russian military presence in Chechnya. In her newspaper columns for *Novaya Gazeta* and her books, *A Small Corner of Hell: Dispatches from Chechnya* and *Putin's Russia*, she detailed the abuse, murders, and torture that took place during the Chechen war and was openly critical of both Putin and the Chechen government. When she was not busy meeting with informants, running from troops and interviewing the war's victims she became the most visible and vocal critic on the topic. That criticism ended abruptly with her assassination on October 7, 2006, by gunshot at the elevator door of her apartment complex. Three years later an associate of Politkovskaya's, a woman journalist named Natalia Estemirova, a specialist on state crimes in Crimea, was kidnapped and shot, her body dumped in some woods.

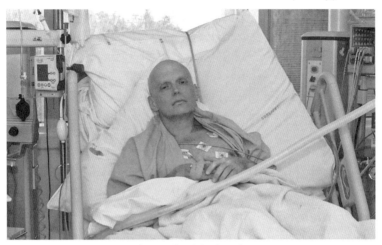

Alexander Litvinenko

## ALEXANDER LITVINENKO

Enter Alexander Litvinenko, one time head of the KGB successor agency, the FSB. Perhaps the least of his accusations against the Putin government was that Putin himself had ordered Anna Politkovska's assassination. He had warned her to escape Russia as he himself had when he fled to the UK and asked for asylum on November 1, 2000, thereafter going to work for British intelligence. Litvinenko had been imprisoned in Russian jails after he allowed several top officers to come forward in 1999 with reports that they had been ordered to assassinate Russian businessman Boris Berezovsky and several others.

Litvinenko proved to be the ultimate conspiracy theorist of Russian affairs. His accusations against Putin's regime included reports that the FSB had trained many Al-Qaeda terrorists, including Ayman al-Zawahiri, Osama Bin Laden's second-in-command. He maintained that Putin was behind an infamous bombing on September 13, 1999 and attendant bombings, including a hostage incident at a Moscow theater in 2002. Russian authorities confiscated thousands of copies of a book Litvinenko wrote on these incidents. Litvinenko also accused Putin of involvement with organized crime and pedophilia. Litvinenko alleged that Romano Prodi, later prime minister of Italy, worked for the KGB and claimed that he had a connection to the notorious

Red Brigade assassination of Aldo Moro.

None of this endeared Litvinenko to the Russian state. He received a warning from a former FSB agent that a special unit had been assigned to assassinate him in2002. He persisted in his criticism of Putin for the next several years, maintaining that Putin came to power by means of an FSB coup and by exacerbating paranoia about terrorism through the various false flag bombings attributed to the Chechnyan separatists.

At lunchtime on November 1, 2006, Litvinenko met with an Italian friend and contact, Mario Scaramella, who had information on the assassination of Anna Politkovska, at the Millennium Hotel's Pine Bar in London. By nightfall Litvinenko was in the hospital, poisoned with the radioactive isotope, most likely delivered via the tea he was served that afternoon.

By November 23, amid much media attention, Litvinenko was dead. His final written message to Vladimir Putin: "You have shown yourself to be barbaric and ruthless as your most hostile critics have claimed. You have shown yourself to have no respect for life, liberty or any civilized value. You have shown yourself to be unworthy of the trust of civilized men and women."

Litvinenko succumbed quickly to the massive dose of Polonium-210 he had ingested in the Millennium Hotel. Previous cases of exposure to the radioactive element had occurred involving Marie Curie's daughter and members of the scientific community in Israel who worked with it in the late 1950s to the 1960s. All of them died of leukemia or other cancers, although none of their deaths could definitely be tracked to exposure the single isotope alone. In any case, those were cases of exposure. Litvinenko had ingested the lethal substance. Toxicologist John Henry, a prominent figure in the investigation of the poisoning of Ukrainian president Viktor Yushchenko, at first attributed the poisoning to thallium, but tests ultimately demonstrated the cause as the far more rare Polonium-210, found virtually exclusively in state-run nuclear reactors and radio isotope laboratories.

Panic ensued in London as traces of the deadly substance were found in a trail across the city, and the authorities ran tests on all those who had contact with Litvinenko at the sushi bar. Radioactive traces were found in a dozen places in London and on two British Airways planes. Litvinenko's wife Mariana and his contact Mario Scaramella both tested positive for small doses of the substance but neither developed any symptoms of poisoning.

Theories moved in many directions. Some suggested that Litvinenko, a Muslim, actually had been caught up in a terrorist attempt to smuggle nuclear materials. Others theorized that Litvinenko's death itself was a false flag operation carried out by Russia's Yuko oil barons to help alleviate legal problems brought on by Putin. The acting president of the Chechen republic claimed that the exiled billionaire Boris Berezovsky had Litvinenko killed in order to weaken the Russian state.

In January 2016 an official inquiry into Litvinenko's death by the British government concluded that Vladimir Putin most likely had direct involvement in Litvinenko's assassination. British Prime Minister David Cameron characterized the conclusion as an appalling example of state sponsored murder. The finding came amidst diplomatic efforts to encourage Russia to aid in ending the conflict in Syria, so Moscow suffered little retaliation other than Cameron's observation that the effort over Syria would be done with "clear eyes and a cold heart."

David Cameron

Paul Klebnikov

## PAUL KLEBNIKOV

The editor of the Russian language edition of *Forbes*, Paul Klebnikov, was killed in a drive-by shooting. He had published lists of Russia's wealthiest and had exposed their corruption in the magazine.

Sergei Yushenkov after being shot.

SERGEI YUSHENKOV

Sergei Yushenkov worked as a Russian policeman and was gathering evidence about Putin involvement in the bombing of an apartment complex in 2004. He was shot in the chest shortly after his political party, Liberal Russia, gained official recognition from the Justice Ministry.

Paul Klebnikov with a Russian edition of *Forbes*.

Paul Joyal

## PAUL JOYAL

Paul Joyal provided the example of the Russian-US parapolitcal nexus. Joval was an expert on Russia's covert intelligence world who had served as a staff member of the US Select Senate Committee on Intelligence. On February 26, 2007 he told the TV news show *Dateline NBC* that Litvinenko's murder served as a signal from Putin's regime as to what would become of its critics. Joyal told the NBC reporter: "A message has been communicated to anyone who wants to speak out against the Kremlin: if you do, no matter who you are, where you are, we will find you and we will silence you in the most horrible way possible." On Thursday March 1, 2007, Joyal was shot and wounded by two men outside of his home in the normally peaceful suburb of Adelphi, Maryland outside of Washington DC.

## VIKTOR YUSHCHENKO

From 2005 to 2010 Viktor Yushchenko served as president of Ukraine. Charges of election fraud against his opponent in the 2004 election led to an election run-off that put Yushchenko in power after a protest movement that led to citizens occupying Independence Square in Kiev. This became known as the country's "Orange Revolution." During the 2004 campaign Yushchenko was poisoned with a powerful toxin called *tetrachlorodibenzodioxin*. The poison caused severe facial disfigurement from which

Viktor Yushchenko

Yushchenko ultimately recovered. The political struggles in Ukraine became more severe when the Russian military seized control of the Ukrainian territory of Crimea, annexing it shortly thereafter.

## VIKTOR YANUKOVYCH

Viktor Yanukovych became president of Ukraine in February 2010 and served for four years. Charges of voter fraud and intimidation not only undermined his first bid for the office in 2004 but resulted in the rioting and occupation event at Independence Square known as the Orange Revolution. Similar protests and demonstrations spread to cities throughout Ukraine. As a result, the Ukrainian Supreme Court nullified the results of the election and a second one brought to power Viktor Yushchenko. Despite his poisoning, Yushchenko served his term and Yanukovych only became president in 2010 after an internationally monitored election. As noted, Yanukovych served for four years.

Yanukovych's presidency came to an end after he reneged on a pledge to sign an agreement associating Ukraine with the European Union. Instead, he signed loan agreements and a treaty

Viktor Yanukovych

with Russia. Rioting once again broke out in Kiev and throughout Ukraine. Called the "Euromaidan movement," this time citizen protesters were met with military force. The escalating clashes caused such furor that Yanukovych was forced to flee to Russia, where he remains.

## MALAYSIAN AIRLINES FLIGHT 17

On July 17, 2014, pro-Putin Ukrainian terrorists launched a surface-to-air missile at a passenger jet flying over eastern Ukraine, en route to Kuala Lumpur from Amsterdam. The resulting explosion and crash killed 298 people, one of the worst shootdowns in aviation history. An investigation by the Dutch concluded that Russian forces had moved the missile into place on the day of the crash and returned it to Russia afterwards. Russia later vetoed a United Nations Security Council effort to prosecute the responsible parties. (Malaysia Airlines suffered a similar disaster four months earlier with the mysterious disappearance of Flight 370 over the South China Sea.)

The press in Russia came up with several conspiracy theories concerning the downing of Flight 17. Separatists at first claimed they had shot down a Ukrainian military plane. When this proved untrue the separatists disowned any responsibility. The television station Russia Today suggested that the incident was an attempt to assassinate Vladimir Putin. Russian media sources also alternately attributed the shootdown to a mistake, a redirect of the flight into a war zone, and to a false flag operation. Reporter Sara Firth resigned from her job with Russia Today in protest over the station's dishonest coverage.

Vladimir Kara-Murza

## VLADIMIR KARA-MURZA

Two attempts were made against the life of Vladimir Kara-Murza, a dissident Russian politician and journalist. Kara-Murza, in tandem with fellow dissident Boris Nemtsov, supported the Magnitsky Act, which passed in the US Congress in 2012. Named after a lawyer in Moscow who was imprisoned, tortured and left to die after he exposed tax fraud in Russia, the act prevented the issuance of visas to anyone involved in Magnitsky's death and other assassinations, corrupt practices and human rights violations. The act led to the forfeiture of many Russian assets in the US. Kara-Murza and Nemtsov prompted versions of the Magnitsky legislation also in Canada and the European Union. In May 2015 Kara-Murza took ill from poisoning after a lunch meeting in Moscow and fell into a coma. He was hospitalized but recovered. In February of 2017 he developed the poisoning symptoms again, returned to the hospital and had to be put into a medically induced coma before recovering a second time.

Boris Nemtsov

## BORIS NEMTSOV

On February 27, 2015, one day prior to a scheduled protest march against the war in the Ukraine, the Russian dissident Boris Nemtsov was shot several times and killed by an unidentified assassin. Nemtsov was a liberal statesman who helped introduce capitalism to post-Soviet Russia. He was a harsh Putin critic and opponent of Russia's military intervention in the Ukraine. His murder by over a half-dozen gunshots occurred near the Kremlin after Nemtsov and his 23-year-old girlfriend, unharmed in the attack, were out after dinner. Too coincidentally, the attack took place in an area where security cameras had been turned off for maintenance.

Russian authorities arrested five suspects and a sixth blew himself up to avoid capture. The remaining five were put on trial by a military court but as of April 2017 verdicts had not been rendered. Investigators indicated that the chief suspect in the murder was a member of a Chechen police unit. It is more likely that the actual killer was never arrested. A municipal truck blocked the one long-distance camera that did record at the time. It all suggested a sophisticated, choreographed cover-up of the crime.

In February 2017 thousands of protesters marched in the streets of Moscow, St. Petersburg and Nizhny Novgorod, Nemtsov's hometown, to observe the second anniversary of the assassination.

## DENIS VORONENKOV

Voronenkov was a former member of the Russian parliament who moved to Ukraine and became a Putin critic. He was shot and killed in the street of Kiev on March 23, 2017. The murder happened simultaneously with a powerful explosion at a Ukrainian ammunitions plant that forcied a mass evacuation of the city of Kharkiv. The current Ukrainian president, Petro O. Poroshenko, asserted that the two events (Voronenkov's murder and the plant explosion) were "no coincidence" and signaled the ongoing nature of the assassination program against Putin's critics. Voronenkov was set to testify in the criminal case against former Ukrainian president Viktor Yanukovych. Voronenkov was married to Bolshoi ballet singer Maria Maksakova.

Denis Voronenkov with Maria Maksakova

Denis Voronenkov after being shot.

## PAUL MANAFORT

The chairman of Donald Trump's presidential campaign also served as a lobbyist for Viktor Yanukovych. He ascended to his position with the Trump campaign after Trump fired his previous manager in April 2016 and was immediately put in charge of a greatly expanded campaign budget. The previous manager, Corey Lewandowski, was brought to court after charges that he forcefully grabbed a woman reporter working for Breitbart News—now often described as Donald Trump's *Pravda*—although the incident ostensibly had no bearing on the power struggle that ended in Manafort replacing him.

A member of Ukraine's parliament attempted to blackmail Manafort by threatening to expose his (and Trump's) connections to Viktor Yanukovyich and Vladimir Putin. Manafort's daughter received a text from parliamentarian Serhiy Leshchenko, denied by him, that allegedly read, "I need to get in touch with Paul. I need to share some important information with him regarding Ukraine investigation. As soon as he comes back to me I will pass you documents. If I don't get any reply from you I am going pass it on to the FBI and Ukrainian authorities inducing media." The text had an accompanying note that read, "Considering all the

Paul Manafort

facts and evidence that are in my possession, and before possible decision whether to pass this to [the National Anti-Corruption Bureau of Ukraine] or FBI I would like to get your opinion on this and maybe your way to work things out that will persuade me to do otherwise."

Manafort remains under investigation by five federal police agencies, including the CIA and the FBI. These investigations include his association with Yanukovyich co-hort Konstantin Kilimnik. Kilimnik flew to the US in 2016 for the Republican National Convention, where he worked to develop the party's new platform of more favorable US-Russian relations. Other members of Trump's campaign met with Russian ambassador Sergey Kislyak at that convention.

Manafort counts among his associates Roger Stone, who confessed online to helping establish backchannel communications between the Trump campaign and Julian Assange to leak disparaging information about Hillary Clinton onto WikiLeaks. Stone had been Trump's liaison with the *National Enquirer* in producing stories about Ted Cruz's sexual affairs during the campaign. Previously, Stone worked as a manager for the hooker in the Eliot Spitzer prostitution scandal and had been banned from CNN and MSNBC for using racist slurs and vulgar language. Less clear is Manafort's association with Carter Page, the Trump foreign

89

policy advisor suspected by intelligence of working with Russian officials sanctioned by the US, whose name figures prominently in the infamous Trump "golden showers" dossier.

## ALPHA BANK

Odd communication between a Russian bank called Alpha Bank and a server at Trump Tower raised a proverbial red flag for computer researchers. Malware investigators discovered a large number of domain name system inquiries between the two entities. A technique called domain name system (DNS) tunneling allows for secret communication to pass through such inquiries. A great deal of communication may have passed between Trump's organization and the Russian government that would be difficult to discover let alone decode, allowing for a potentially extraordinary level of covert coordination.

## GUCCIFER 2.0

An entity called Guccifer 2.0 takes the credit for the hacks of the computer network of the Democratic National Committee. Leaks from that cyber-crime to Julian Assange's WikiLeaks and to the media at large makeup the central activity concerning Russian manipulation of the 2016 US election. Actual information revealed by the links came mixed with the usual stew of conspiracizing. US intelligence services determined that two Russian spy groups comprised Guccifer 2.0. Designated "APT 28" and "APT 29" (APT = "Advances Persistent Threat") the groups traced back to the GRU, the foreign military intelligence agency of the General Staff of the Armed Forces of the Russian Federation.

The name "Guccifer" combines "the style of Gucci and the light of Lucifer" according to the man who coined it, Marcel Lazar Lehel. A hacker from Romania, Lehel was the original Guccifer, responsible for breaks into computer accounts of George Bush's sister. Known also for hacking the accounts of Romanian officials, Lehel was extradited to the US, indicted on federal charges in the US courts and was sentenced to 52 months in prison.

The extent of Donald Trump's entanglements with the Russian oligarchy, the murderous state bureaucracy and its cyber-espionage skullduggery had not fully unraveled in public as of his administration's third month. He continued to withhold from public disclosure of his tax returns, which would have identified at least some of these connections. In 2008, for instance, he sold a Palm Beach mansion property at 215 North County Road to Dmitry Rybolovlev, a Russian oligarch, for $95 million—$13 million more than any Palm Beach mansion had sold previously. That Rybolovley's jet shadowed Trump's during the 2016 campaign and twice wound up in the same airport Rybolovlev attributed to coincidence. MSNBC's Rachel Maddow obtained Trump's tax return from 2005 but it did not include attachments with potential information about Trump's financial dealings with Russians. The emasculated form had "Client Copy" stamped on it, suggesting that Trump himself had a hand in producing the misleading document.

Congressional hearings investigating the connections between Donald Trump and the Russians began on March 20, 2017. The ranking Democrat on the House Intelligence Committee charged with this inquiry, Representative Adam Schiff of California's 28th Congressional District, summarized the conspiratorial trail in the most comprehensive manner to that date:

"The months of July and August 2016 appear to have been pivotal.

It was at this time the Russians began using the information they had stolen to help Donald Trump and harm Hillary Clinton. And so the question is, why? What was happening in July, August of last year and were U.S. persons involved?

Here are some of the matters drawn from public sources alone since that is all we can discuss in this setting that concern us and we believe should concern all Americans.

In early July, Carter Page, someone candidate Trump identified as one of his national security advisors, travels to Moscow on a trip approved by the Trump campaign. While in Moscow, he gives a speech critical of the United States and other western countries

Carter Page

for what he believes is a hypocritical focus on democratization and efforts to fight corruption.

According to Christopher Steele, a British—a former British intelligence officer, who is reportedly held in high regard by U.S. intelligence, Russian sources tell him that Page has also had a secret meeting with Igor Sechin, CEO of the Russian gas giant, Rosneft. Sechin is reported to be a former KGB agent and close friend of Putin's.

According to Steele's Russian sources, Page is offered brokerage fees by such on a deal involving a 19 percent share of the company. According to Reuters, the sale of a 19.5 percent share of Rosneft later takes place with unknown purchasers and unknown brokerage fees. Also, according to Steele's Russian sources, the campaign has offered documents damaging to Hillary Clinton which the Russians would publish through an outlet that gives them deniability like WikiLeaks.

The hacked documents would be in exchange for a Trump administration policy that de-emphasizes Russia's invasion of Ukraine and instead focuses on criticizing NATO countries for not paying their fair share. Policies which even as recently as the President's meeting last week with Angela Merkel have now presently come to pass. In the middle of July, Paul Manafort, the—the Trump campaign manager and someone who was long on the payroll of Pro Russian-Ukrainian interests attends the

Russian—the Republican Party Convention. Carter Page, back from Moscow, also attends the convention. According to Steele, it was Manafort who chose Page to serve as a go-between for the Trump campaign and Russian interests.

Ambassador Kislyak, who presides over a Russian Embassy in which diplomatic personnel would later be expelled as likely spies, also attends the Republican Party Convention and meets with Carter Page, and additional Trump advisors J.D. Gordon and Walid Phares. It was J.D. Gordon who approved Page's trip to Moscow.

Ambassador Kislyak also meets with Trump national campaign chair, National Security Campaign Chair and now attorney general, Jeff Sessions. Sessions would later deny meeting with Russian officials during his Senate confirmation hearing. Just prior to the convention, the Republican Party platform is changed, removing a section that supports the provision of lethal defensive weapons to Ukraine, an action that would be contrary to Russian interests.

Manafort categorically denies involvement by the Trump campaign and altering the platform, but the Republican Party delegate who offered the language in support of providing defensive weapons to Ukraine states it was removed at the insistence of the Trump campaign. Later, J.D. Gordon admits opposing the inclusion of the provision at the time it was being debated and prior to its being removed.

Jeff Sessions

Later in July and after the convention, the first stolen emails detrimental to Hillary Clinton appear on WikiLeaks. A hacker who goes by the moniker Guccifer 2.0 claims responsibility for hacking the DNC and giving the documents to WikiLeaks. Leading private cyber security firms including Crowdstrike, Mandiant and ThreatConnect review the evidence of the hack and conclude with high certainty that it was the work of APT 28 and APT 29 who are known to be Russian intelligence services.

The U.S. intelligence committee also later confirms that the documents were in fact stolen by Russian intelligence and Guccifer 2.0 acted as a front. Also in late July, candidate Trump praises WikiLeaks, says he loves them and openly appeals to the Russians to hack his opponent's emails telling them that they will be richly rewarded by the press.

On August 8th, Roger Stone, a long time Trump political advisor and self-proclaimed political dirty trickster, boasts in his speech that he has communicated with Assange and that more documents would be coming, including an October surprise. In the middle of August, he also communicates with the Russian cut out Guccifer 2.0 and authors a *Breitbart* piece denying Guccifer's links to Russian intelligence.

Then later in August, Stone does something truly remarkable when he predicts that John Podesta's personal emails will soon be published, trust me he says, it will soon be Podesta's time in

Roger Stone

Sergey Kislyak

the barrel, *#crookedHillary*. In the weeks that follow, Stone shows remarkable prescience. I have total confidence that WikiLeaks and my hero, Julian Assange will educate the American people soon, he says, #LockHerUp. Payload coming, he predicts and two days later it does.

WikiLeaks releases its first batch of Podesta emails. The release of John Podesta's emails would then continue on a daily basis, up until the election. On Election Day in November, Donald Trump wins. Donald Trump appoints one of his high-profile surrogates, Michael Flynn, to be his national security advisor. Michael Flynn has been paid by the Kremlin's propaganda outfit RT in the past, as well as another Russian entity.

In December, Michael Flynn has a secret conversation with Ambassador Kislyak, about sanctions imposed by President Obama on Russia over attacking [the US election through the e-mail hacking] designed to help the Trump campaign. Michael Flynn lies about the secret conversation. The vice president unknowingly then assures the country that no—no such conversation ever happened. The president is informed that Flynn has lied and Pence has misled the country. The president does nothing.

Two weeks later, the press reveals that Flynn has lied and the president is forced to fire Mr. Flynn. The president then praises the man who lied, Mr. Flynn, and castigates the press for exposing the lie.

Now, is it possible that the removal of the Ukraine provision

Michael Flynn

from the GOP platform was a coincidence? Is it a coincidence that Jeff Sessions failed to tell the Senate about his meetings with a Russian ambassador, not only at the convention, but a more private meeting in his office and at a time when the U.S. election was under attack by the Russians?

Is it a coincidence that Michael Flynn would lie about a conversation he had with the same Russian Ambassador Kislyak, about the most pressing issue facing both countries at the time they spoke, the U.S. imposition of sanctions over Russian hacking of our election designed to help Donald Trump? Is it a coincidence that the Russian gas company, Rosneft, sold a 19 percent share after former British intelligence officer Steele was told by Russian sources that Carter Page was offered fees on a deal of just that size?

Is it a coincidence that Steele's Russian sources also affirmed that Russia had stolen documents hurtful to Secretary Clinton that it would utilize in exchange for Pro Russian policies that would later come to pass? Is it a coincidence that Roger Stone predicted that John Podesta would be a victim of a Russian hack and have his private emails published and did so even before Mr. Podesta himself, was fully aware that his private emails would be exposed?

Is it possible that all of these events and reports are completely unrelated and nothing more than an entirely unhappy coincidence? Yes, it is possible. But it is also possible, maybe more than possible, that they are not coincidental, not disconnected and not unrelated and that the Russians use the same techniques to corrupt U.S. persons that they employed in Europe and elsewhere. We simply don't know, not yet. And we owe it to the country to find out." (End quote from Adam Schiff)

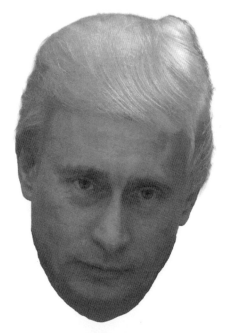

Vladimir Trump

## TRUMPOCALYPSE REVELATIONS
### Four Horsemen

Reince Priebus, Chief of Staff: a Trump critic during the campaign, described in one newspaper as "small and unimpressive... bitter and whiny."

Steve Bannon, Chief Strategist: rightist ideologue from *Breitbart News*, he nevertheless spent 1993 to 1995 as part of the eco-friendly, space flaky *Biosphere 2* project in Oracle, Arizona.

Rex Tillerson, Secretary of State: former CEO of ExxonMobil, no previous government experience, no previous meeting with Trump.

Sean Spicer, Press Secretary: now indistinguishable from the *Saturday Night Live* parody done by performer Melissa McCarthy.

*Left*: Sean Spicer. *Right*: Melissa McCarthy as Spicer.

| 1995 | **Resident Income Tax Return** | IT-201 |
|---|---|---|

New York State ● City of New York ● City of Yonkers

For the year January 1 through December 31, 1995, or fiscal tax year beginning _____ , 1995 ending _____ , 19 _____

**For office use only**

| Last name | First name and middle initial (if joint return, enter both names) | Your social security no. |
|---|---|---|
| TRUMP, DONALD J. AND MARLA | | |

| Mailing address (number and street or rural route) | Apartment number | Spouse's social sec. no. |
|---|---|---|
| 721 FIFTH AVENUE | | |

| City, village or post office | State | ZIP code | New York State county of residence |
|---|---|---|---|
| NEW YORK | NY | 10022 | ● NEW YORK |

In the space below, print or type your permanent home address within New York State if it is not the same as your mailing address above (see instructions, page 25).

School district name: ● MANHATTAN

| Permanent home address (number and street or rural route) | Apartment number |
|---|---|
| | School district code number .......... 369 |

| City, village or post office | State | ZIP code | If taxpayer is deceased, enter first name and date of death. |
|---|---|---|---|
| | NY | | |

**(A) Filing status** - mark an "X" in one box

(1) Single

(2) X Married filing joint return (enter spouse's social security number above)

(3) Married filing separate return (enter spouse's social security number above)

(4) Head of household (with qualifying person)

(5) Qualifying widow(er) with dependent child

Clip check or money order here.

**(B)** Did you itemize your deductions on your 1995 federal income tax return? ▮ Yes X ▮ No

**(C)** Can you be claimed as a dependent on another taxpayer's federal return? ▮ Yes ▮ No X

**(D)** If you do not need forms mailed to you next year, mark an "X" in the box (see instructions) ...... ▮ X

**(E)** Enter the number of exemptions claimed from your federal return, line 6e .................... 3

**Federal Income and Adjustments**

For lines 1 through 17 below, enter your income items and total adjustments as they appear on your federal return (see page 14). See instructions on page 14 for showing a loss.

| | | | Dollars | Cents |
|---|---|---|---|---|
| 1 | Wages, salaries, tips, etc. | 1. | 6,108 | . |
| 2 | Taxable interest income | 2. | 7,386,825 | . |
| 3 | Dividend income | 3. | 26,051 | . |
| 4 | Taxable refunds, credits, or offsets of state and local income taxes (also enter on line 23 below) | 4. | 62,205 | . |
| 5 | Alimony received | 5. | | . |
| 6 | Business income or loss (attach copy of federal Schedule C or C-EZ, Form 1040) | 6. | 3,427,092 | . |
| 7 | Capital gain or loss (if required, attach copy of federal Schedule D, Form 1040) | 7. | -3,000 | . |
| 8 | Other gains or losses (attach copy of federal Form 4797) | 8. | -1,356,097 | . |
| 9 | Taxable amount of IRA distributions | 9. | | . |
| 10 | Taxable amount of pensions and annuities | 10. | | . |
| 11 | Rental real estate, royalties, partnerships, S corporations, trusts, etc. (attach copy of federal Sch. E, Form 1040) | 11. | -15,818,562 | . |
| 12 | Farm income or loss (attach copy of federal Schedule F, Form 1040) | 12. | | . |
| 13 | Unemployment compensation | 13. | | . |
| 14 | Taxable amount of social security benefits (also enter on line 25 below) | 14. | | . |
| 15 | Other income (see page 14) SEE STATEMENT 1 | 15. | -909,459,915 | . |
| 16 | Add lines 1 through 15 | 16. | -915,729,293 | . |
| 17 | Total federal adjustments to income (see page 14) | 17. | -------- | - |
| 18 | Subtract line 17 from line 16. This is your federal adjusted gross income | 18. | -915,729,293 | . |

**New York Additions:** (see page 15)

| 19 | Interest income on state and local bonds and obligations (but not those of NY State or its local governments) | 19. | | . |
|---|---|---|---|---|
| 20 | Public employee 414(h) retirement contributions from your wage and tax statements (see page 15) | 20. | | . |
| 21 | Other (see page 15) SEE STATEMENT 2 | 21. | 43,371,489 | . |
| 22 | Add lines 18 through 21 | 22. | -872,357,804 | . |

**New York Subtractions:** (see page 17)

| 23 | Taxable refunds, credits, or offsets of state & local income taxes (line 4 above) | 23. | 62,205 | . |
|---|---|---|---|---|
| 24 | Pensions of NYS and local governments and the federal government (see page 17) | 24. | | . |
| 25 | Taxable amount of social security benefits (from line 14 above) | 25. | | . |
| 26 | Interest income on US government bonds | 26. | | . |
| 27 | Pension and annuity income exclusion | 27. | | . |
| 28 | Other (see page 17) SEE STATEMENT 3 | 28. | 41,345,875 | . |
| 29 | Add lines 23 through 28 | 29. | 41,408,080 | . |
| 30 | Subtract line 29 from line 22. This is your New York adjusted gross income (enter the line 30 amount on line 31 on the back page.) | 30. | -913,765,884 | . |

021507      IT-201 1995

Trump's tax return from 1995

# Chapter 8

# Alternative Theories

"…not a Chain of single Links, for one broken Link could lose us All,— rather, a great disorderly Tangle of Lines, long and short, weak and strong, vanishing into the Mnemonick Deep, with only their Destination in common."
—Thomas Pynchon

No small irony attends the fact that the rightist populism of Donald Trump's presidency is beset with suspicions of Russian influence. Since the 1950s followers of the leftism of Beatniks and hippies as well as the politically active left had been characterized as dupes and pawns of Soviet Russia. The word Beatnik, in fact, as Abbie Hoffman often pointed out, was a red smear derived from the Sputnik satellite. "Peaceniks" and "Nogoodniks" populated the pages of political satire of the time. The Soviets did, in fact, infiltrate and propagate these groups and there was no shortage of McCarthyist politicians to capitalize on that reality and those fears. And so with the Trumpniks, many of them genuine mom-and-populists uncomfortable with and suspicious of the more recent American multiculturalism and globalism. Some, however, also were aided by Russian propaganda to view themselves as rebels against the New World Order and the Deep State—a Trump administration term for the lingering bureaucratic constructs of the Obama reign.

Trump's rise to power came in no small part due to the unmanageability of the media spectacle. Trump's every supposed misstep captivated his audience and the television cameras more and more. The news networks could not turn away, providing the candidate with uncountable dollars in free media exposure resources by devoting their airtime to his political rallies. Late-night talk show comedians could not turn their eyes away either, even as the culture of ridicule became an obvious instrument of Donald Trump's success. The New York newspapers daily featured Trump in clown white. Trump had strengths of popular interest totally belied by the sliver of older, white, non-college-educated voters, the alienated Rust Belt, that came to the polls for him.

During the primary season leftist pundits delighted in how Trump decimated the older ranks of the Republicans, particularly the Bush family, longtime players in the annals of conspiracy theory. The same with the Clintons, also viewed by many as a conspiratorial crime syndicate. Trump wiped the slate clean of conspiracy bugaboos that beleaguered the thoughtful for generations. On the strength of that alone he earned an undying following, impervious to whatever ignorance or malevolence he expressed, even as it worked against the best interests of those who held the view.

Trump also expanded the ranks of conspiracists by converting a large majority of the Democratic party, its political fortunes now tied to the still unfolding parapolitics of the Russian connection. This group followed in earnest the diminishing fortunes of Michael Flynn, forced to resign as Trump's national security adviser after discovery that he had lied to Vice President Pence about his relationship with Russian ambassador Sergey Kislyak. The idea of "wiretapping," an archaic term for surveillance, became less of an issue in relation to Flynn than it did when Trump started making similar accusations that he had been "wire-tapped" by Obama. This sort of discourse—a battle of conspiracy theories—became central to the public discussion and celebrated by Trump supporters.

A counterconspiracy, pro-Trump theory had circulated about Michael Flynn prior to his resignation, from a source familiar to conspiracy readers. Thierry Meyssan, the French author of a well-known screed on 9/11 entitled *L'Effroyable imposture (The Big Lie),* reported that Flynn had plans to "override all post 9/11 reforms. This would put an end to the obsession with secret prisons and targeted assassinations and mark a return to the true nature of intelligence: making sense of and anticipating developments around the world." Meyssan's 9/11 theory had argued that the events of that day were orchestrated by US military industrialists. Elsewhere he suggested that the plane that hit the Pentagon that day was, in fact, a missile. Elsewhere, Meyssan had become quite the supporter of Donald Trump, telling one interviewer, "In the West, with the anti-Trump campaign, we are just entering the first phase of propaganda itself. Because this is the first time the system has attacked the Presidency which it claimed to be supreme. On this occasion, there is a contradiction between the techniques of public relations and those of propaganda. Indeed, Donald Trump is a specialist of the former and a victim of the latter." Few critics went that far, although others noted the short interval between Flynn's resignation and the emergence of the surveillance recording of him—clearly a dirty trick to forestall Flynn's reforms.

Meyssan presented a more elaborate view of Flynn's potential reforms. Flynn planned "placing all 16 Intelligence agencies under the exclusive authority of a Director of National Intelligence, supposed to supervise information sharing" and "abolishing the line between agents on the ground and analysts in favor of functional centers such as the ones we see in the TV series 24." Meyssan did not make it clear whether or not this last reference to a television spectacle was his inference or Flynn's idea. Meyssan continues, "the Director of National Intelligence clearly had the power to centralize intelligence which until then had been dispersed, but he lacked the power to interfere with how the different agencies were operating. So for example, he did not have the power to remove an incompetent officer... the current functional centers excel in providing information instantly. They are able to pinpoint an individual anywhere in the world and, if need be, eliminate him. But this is not Intelligence. The correct term is crime. Even if the CIA miraculously topples the regimes that the White House disapproves of and sets up secret prisons, it is not by any measure more knowledgeable on anticipating political developments, and to a lesser extent still, military developments." It remains unclear how much of this is author Meyssan's interpretation and how much it reflected Flynn's actual thinking.

In any event, Flynn became history after his forced resignation. While Flynn was waiting to be called to testify before Congress about the Russian-Trump connection, the *National Enquirer*—Donald Trump's newspaper of record, which had floated stories about Ted Cruz's extramarital affairs and link to the JFK assassination—reported that Trump himself outed Flynn as a Russian spy. "The revelations come as still unfolding," reports the *Enquirer*, "details continue to worm their way into the public eye about Trump's own White House turncoat—now ousted national security adviser and retired Lt. Gen. Michael Flynn."

The Enquirer story continued:

> Flynn was booted from Trump's cabinet after intercepted phone calls exposed how he had colluded with Russian officials—and then had the *chutzpah* to lie about it when questioned by Vice President Mike Pence. "He was in essence, Russian spy in Trump's midst," said an administration source who spoke to the Enquirer on the condition of anonymity. "Trump was lucky to root him out when he did. The unfolding Russian spy drama will overshadow the House of Representatives…"

Between Meyssan and the *Enquirer,* Flynn became romanticized and demonized; Donald Trump remained idolized from both perspectives, and the real Mikael Flynn remained in the shadows, considering his options. In late March 2017, the *Wall Street Journal* reported that Michael Flynn was seeking immunity from prosecution in exchange for testifying before the congressional Russian investigation committee. His lawyer tried to make granting immunity seem like a good idea, teasing the committee with the statement: "General Flynn certainly has a story to tell, and he very much wants to tell it…" This hints that the person(s) his testimony would implicate might be very high placed, indeed. Some viewed the *National Enquirer* story, a clear attempt by Trump to throw Flynn under the bus, as part of the impetus for Flynn's turning whistleblower.

Trump famously had told a press conference in Doral, Florida in July 2016 that he hoped Russian intelligence had hacked Hillary Clinton's e-mails and would publish the stolen material. "Russia, if you're listening, I hope you're able to find the 30,000 emails that are missing. I think you will probably be rewarded mightily by our press." The press instead reported the remarks as encouraging an enemy to perform high-tech espionage on his own country. The exhortation came amidst reporting that Russia had hacked the Democratic National Committee's computer servers in support of Trump's campaign—the central issue that dogged his early presidency.

Yet, the Clinton e-mail issue involved 30,000 e-mails Hillary Clinton erased from a private server while under federal investigation. Under the umbrella of the Clinton Global Initiative, Clinton received kickbacks for international uranium sales. She had been using the same server for slush fund operations, paying personal consultant Huma Abedin, funding a $34,000 a night Caribbean vacation for daughter Chelsea and giving payoffs to silence Bill Clinton's sex accusers. Those crimes were cybercrimes more serious than any by the likes of such notorious cybercriminals as Edward Snowden or Julian Assange.

Even as the Trump-Russia connection blossomed into a congressional investigation, Trump supporters considered the case for it weak, but even if true not such a bad thing. From this perspective, Putin was on the right side of the issues in the first place: the US was pushing for illegal but openly stated policies of regime change in Ukraine and Syria; Putin is a foe of the international pedophilia networks; and Putin rightly opposed Genetically Modified Organisms (GMOs). Alternately, the US only pretends to fights ISIS; the Syrian war was caused by the US and NATO acting on behalf of the worst players in the Middle East; and the neocon leadership wants war with Russia.

All of this was growing out of the historic backdrop of eight years of Barack Obama, who as a kid was a Muslim in Indonesia and called himself a Muslim on one occasion; whose mother at one time belonged to a crypto-Muslim cult; and who was putting Muslims in senior government positions. Also in this view, Islam possesses a unique affinity for pedophilia and homosexuality, and Obama was a pedophile victim himself, and gay. Donald Trump, despite his compulsive lying, "pussy grabbing" remarks, and statements about wanting to date his own daughter, was a normal person by comparison.

## TRUMPOCALYPSE REVELATIONS
## A CALENDAR OF TRUMP ADMINISTRATION HIGHLIGHTS

April 2017
4/1
Trump walks out of Oval Office without signing executive orders, flummoxed by press questions about Michael Flynn

4/2
Trump plays golf with Rand Paul

4/3
Senate Judiciary Committee vote on Supreme Court nominee Neil Gorsuch; House Republicans enacted "nuclear option," a parliamentary move to stop a Democratic filibuster

4/5
Trump removes Stephen Bannon from the National Security Council

4/6
Launches 59 Tomahawk cruise missile strike against targets in Syria, without Congressional approval, while eating cake with Xi Jinping, the general secretary of the Chinese Communist Party, at Mar-A-Lago

4/6
Devin Nunes recuses himself from the House Intelligence Committee Russian investigation

4/6
Trump accuses Susan Rice, national security adviser under Obama, of illegally "unmasking"—a legal process—identities of Trump associates in reports from intelligence agencies

4/7
Gorsuch confirmed by Senate

4/10
Gorsuch sworn in

4/11
Press secretary Sean Spicer asserts that Hitler never used chemical weapons and refers to the Nazi death camps as "holocaust centers"

4/11
Trump claims to have sent an armada of aircraft carriers to North Korea

4/12
Reports surface that the FBI obtained secret court orders in Summer 2016 to monitor Trump aide Carter Page, suspecting him to be a Russian agent

4/13
US military drops its most powerful, non-nuclear bomb, a GBU-43/B Massive Ordnance Air Blast Bomb, MOAB, nicknamed "Mother of All Bombs"—on ISIS targets in Afghanistan. Trump does not say if he specifically ordered the bombing.

4/14
Trump makes visitor logs to the White House secret

4/16
Protesters clash in Berkeley, CA, with 13 arrests; Tax Day protests elsewhere over Trump not making his taxes public

4/19
Reports indicate that Trump's aircraft carrier armada was actually headed to Australia, in the opposite direction from North Korea, for training exercises

4/19
"Golden Showers" dossier authenticated in part by the FBI, which says it used the information therein as justification to obtain a wiretap on Carter Page
4/20
Trump pals Sarah Palin, Ted Nugent and Kid Rock strike poses for photos in front of Hillary Clinton's portrait in the White House

4/22
Earth Day—protests at the National Mall and in cities throughout the US against Trump's climate change denial and cuts in science education

4/23
New polls show a three-point drop from the already record low popularity percentage

4/24
"Resist Trump" tickets sold by Food and Water Watch to protest expanded fracking and other Trump environmental policies

4/26
Trump's 100th day in office; protests occur throughout the country

4/27
"Indivisible" movement organizes anti-Trump training event in Austin, TX

4/28
March against Trump's climate policies in Columbus, OH, Washington, DC, NYC and other cities

4/29
Trump appears at rally in Harrisburg, PA, the city where the Three-Mile Island nuclear near-meltdown happened

4/30
Anti-Trump aerobics event held in San Francisco

Trump pals Kid Rock, Sarah Palin, and Ted Nugent strike poses for photos in front of Hillary Clinton's portrait in the White House.

# Chapter 9

# End Times

"I was in the Spirit on the Lord's day,
and heard behind me a great voice, as of a trumpet."
—*Revelation* 1: 10

The comedian Bill Hicks noted that right wing politicians do not get killed by assassinations, they get wounded. Ronald Reagan. George Wallace. The forces of violent death largely unleash themselves on the liberals. The Kennedy brothers. Martin Luther King. The cynical math worked in Trump's favor. If the historic pattern held, Trump likely would survive an assassination attempt. His line of succession went to another right-winger, Mike Pence, and then to Speaker Paul Ryan and then disappeared into the two houses of Congress, both majority Republican.

Opposition to Trump, however, took more the form of nonviolent protest, with mass demonstrations by women; airport traveler activists who clogged airports to protest against Trump's immigration ban; "Not My President" generalists; Trump tax day organizers demanding disclosures; climate change protesters; and many others—although all that was peppered with some violent squirmishes. Trump had eked out a victory in the electoral college. Of the popular vote, 62,976,636 people voted for Donald Trump; his opponent earned 65,844,610 votes. The victory came in the electoral college, where Trump received 304 electoral votes compared to Clinton's 232 (270 needed to win).

It was a technical win in a string of such things pulled off by Republican candidates. George W. Bush gained the office after a Supreme Court decision and controversial ballot recounting in Florida where his brother was coincidently the governor, when every "hanging chad" from the physical ballots became an issue. Ronald Reagan made a deal with enemy Iranians to extend a hostage crisis until his opponent was defeated. The first George Bush had deep CIA connections that went back to the Kennedy assassination. Extra-electoral—parapolitcal—processes attended all of these national elections. Donald Trump stepped into that atmosphere; he didn't create it. Even though he was a particularly inept conspiracy theorist, without a clue about JFK, for instance, but able to take the fog surrounding the assassination and use it politically, he rose to power in a popular culture of unresolved conflict about its political leadership. He carried concepts about the "deep state" and "fake media" to the center of power, even as he employed some of the deepest state players and generated fake news of his own nightly.

By April 2017 the sustainability of Trump's conspiracy triumph remained to be seen. His two attempts at stopping immigration from Muslim majority countries stalled in the courts. His effort to repeal health care reforms made by the previous administration also failed. A filibuster faced his Supreme Court nominee. A serviceman was killed in an al-Qaeda raid in Yemen. Trump's approval rating, 36%, is the lowest ever for the office at this early point in an administration. Media attention shifted from the romance it had with his populist vision during the campaign to obsession over the intricacy of his machinations with the Russians. The Russia thing, also, has become the subject of extensive congressional attention, with key players now poised to give testimony. Michael Flynn sought immunity in exchange for telling his story, which most presumed had to do with Trump trading favors with the Russians—to lift sanctions and soft-pedal Ukraine in exchange for the leaking of John Podesta's e-mails. Trump would be forced to resign, with Vice President Pence waiting in the wings with a pardon, or so went the speculation. Only three months in and Trump's presidency had become more embroiled in conspiracy spectacle than any predecessor. The Trumpocalypse was at hand, no less so for the dammed who must endure it than for the Great Beast himself.

# Afterword:

# On Trumpocalypse Now

How did we get here? How is it possible that a man like Trump could become president? He hardly seems human, but rather what in the Jewish tradition was called a *golem*, a monster created from inanimate matter. The beast was made to defend its creators from the assaults of others. And like the golem of folklore, those who created him became the first targets of attack. Or perhaps he is more like a living invocation of Jack Kirby's Psycho-Man, who had the power to energetically attack the human mind with rays inciting fear, hate, or doubt at varying levels.

In one sense he was inevitable in this culture, and not without precedent—as the author Kenn Thomas points out, there have been other pop culture politicians like Ronald Reagan and Jesse Ventura. Ventura reportedly did a creditable job as governor, and he even pondered a presidential run, with Howard Stern as a running mate. For a more conspiratorial pairing, political comedian Dick Gregory once ran for high office with JFK researcher Mark Lane as his VP pick.

However, one thing that Donald Trump has accomplished as president is to force the United States to look in the mirror. All of the sin and bile from centuries of buried American history have made that reflection ugly indeed. Our instinct is to flinch. We cannot give in to that instinct, as Thomas shows us in this work. Indeed, what Thomas has done in *Trumpocalypse Now* is give a kind of survey course in American parapolitics, using our 45th president as a focus. Drawing from sources including documentary evidence and cultural byproducts (such as television programs), he leads a guided tour of the strange world that birthed our current situation. As with everything in life, there is not one rabbit hole but dozens, and the tunnels rush deep underground and cross in all directions.

And what does "parapolitics" mean? Conspiracy theory? That is one interpretation. But like so many things, it depends on what views you bring to the table. As my mentor John Judge used to say, "Brother, can you paradigm?" What parapolitics supposes, when you get right down to it, is that humans continue to behave in all-too-human ways when they obtain access to power. In other words, rather than serving the political (and often elusive) "will of the people," they tend to *serve themselves*. What Trump has done is remove the pretense of statesmanship from the position and embody pure *rapaciousness*. He appears to serve, without shame, himself. In that sense one must say that Trump is the most honest of presidents, where Obama—radiating smooth intelligence—was one of the least.

During the obscenity trial of William Burroughs's novel *Naked Lunch*, Allen Ginsberg testified that he thought the "naked lunch" of the title was "...the number one World's Health Problem, which, he feels, is this tendency on the part of—the tendency in a mechanized civilization for very few people to get control of enormous amounts of power." That is the story of Western civilization, and Trump fits snugly in a progression of such power, and not the exception as much as the American media would like to pretend.

As I write this, word has come from London of a "terrorist attack" in which four people have been killed by a lone nut. As with all researchers into parapolitics, I mentally prepare for the deluge of information to come. We try to get as many first reports as we can, knowing that the first reports are often the last chance to get the facts before the cover story falls. Will we find that this truly is a lone, unstable individual whose story is an unfortunate one of mental deficiency? Or does a web of connections await to be assembled and constructed from the known details?

Such is life in modern Western society. And no matter the incident, there will always be those who endorse the State, and others who will always propose a Conspiracy. Fewer among their number will be those who will do the *work*, bringing forth the spade to dig in the detritus looking for the truth. Kenn Thomas has spent his life digging, and pointing the way, and allowing others to draw conclusions from the work.

The book is an extraordinary exercise in what academics like to call "multidisciplinary studies," in that the author draws us into the background of the Clinton presidency, the possible Russian connections to Trump, its relation to Majestic-12, along with references to JFK and *Route 66*, and fits it all into a coherent narrative. *Trumpocalypse Now* also reminds us that no matter how well-informed we think we are, none of us has access to the whole picture. In this complicated world, if you think you've got it all figured out, that's a sure sign you haven't. Get some humility and get to digging.

—Joseph E. Green, March 22, 2017
dissentingviews.com

"a people's welfare or misery flows in a stream from their prince,
as from a never-failing spring."
—Thomas More, *Utopia,* Book 1

# Epilogue

# The War Weeks

# by Kenn Thomas

With the cloud of unsettled congressional investigation into his presidential campaign's ties to Russia, Donald Trump moved forward with foreign policy aggression. In the first week of April, he launched a missile strike against Syria. He ordered the launch of fifty-nine Tomahawk cruise missiles from the Mediterranean Sea towards Syria's Sharyat airbase. The declared purpose for the attack was retaliation for the Khan Shaykhun chemical attack of the preceding week. An airstrike by the Syrian government there released sarin gas and other chemical substances, killing 75 civilians and poisoning over 500, including women and children, whose bodies gave graphic testimony on American television broadcasts. The American counterattack served to take the edge off the growing US investigation of the Trump campaign's ties to Russia by making the new administration look tough against the Russians by bombing its ally Syria. Shortly after the strike, however, news emerged that the Trump administration had warned Russian authorities in advance to avoid the risk of killing any Russian military personnel.

Trump got aggressive again when he ordered what he described as an "armada" to the Sea of Japan, the waters around North Korea. This supposedly was done in response to the continued nuclear ballistic missile program of North Korean dictator Kim Jung Un. Trump declared that he had dispatched the aircraft carrier *USS Carl Vinson* and its accompanying strike group. The White House later declared that declaration to be an "erroneous" miscommunication with the White House. However, the Vincent group actually was deployed 3,500 miles away conducting long-scheduled joint exercises in the Indian Ocean with the Royal Australian Navy. The false announcement only inflamed the already dangerously tense situation on the Korean peninsula.

Next came the MOAB—the "mother of all bombs"—also known as the Massive Ordnance Air Blast Bomb, the GBU-43/B. The largest explosive device in the US arsenal short of a nuclear bomb, US forces unloaded it on a target in Afghanistan, the series of underground tunnels near the Pakistan border that harbored a population of ISIS fighters. Thirty-six ISIS fighters died in the attack. It was the most successful of Trump's foreign policy muscle flexing exercises but, alas, not ordered by Trump as it turned out. The order came from a commander on the ground. Trump nevertheless kept it vague in public statements.

In this atmosphere, two Russian TU-95 Bear bombers were tracked flying over forty miles off the coast of Alaska just after two US-F22 fighter jets intercepted similar Russian aircraft in the area. That's where foreign relations stood in the springtime at the dawn of the Trumpocalypse, amidst a militarism clouded by Russian connections and clouded also by miscommunication and disinformation from Donald Trump's White House.

# Appendix:

# The "Golden Showers" Dossier

The following dossier surfaced in the American media on January 10, 2017. British MI6 agent Christopher Steele claims credit for authorship. The date of each report is at the end of each report.

COMPANY INTELLIGENCE REPORT 2016/080

US PRESIDENTIAL ELECTION: REPUBLICAN CANDIDATE DONALD TRUMP'S

ACTIVITIES IN RUSSIA AND COMPROMISING RELATIONSHIP WITH THE KREMLIN

Summary

-Russian regime has been cultivating, supporting and assisting TRUMP for at least 5 years. Aim, endorsed by PUTIN, has been to encourage splits and divisions in western alliance

-So far TRUMP has declined various sweetener real estate business deals offered him in Russia in order to further the Kremlin's cultivation of him. However he and his inner circle have accepted a regular flow of intelligence from the Kremlin, including on his Democratic and other political rivals

-Former top Russian intelligence officer claims FSB has compromised TRUMP through his activities in Moscow sufficiently to be able to blackmail him. According to several knowledgeable sources, his conduct in Moscow has included perverted sexual acts which have been arranged/monitored by the FSB

-A dossier of compromising material on Hillary CLINTON has been collated by the Russian Intelligence Services over many years and mainly comprises bugged conversations she had on various visits to Russia and intercepted phone calls rather than any embarrassing conduct. The

dossier is controlled by Kremlin spokesman, PESKOV, directly on orders. However it has not as yet been distributed abroad, including to TRUMP. Russian intentions for its deployment still unclear

Detail

1. Speaking to a trusted compatriot in June 2016 sources A and B, a senior Russian Foreign Ministry figure and a former top level Russian intelligence officer still active inside the Kremlin respectively said, the Russian authorities had been cultivating and supporting US Republican presidential candidate Donald TRUMP for at least 5 years. Source asserted that the TRUMP operation was both supported and directed by Russian President Vladimir PUTIN. Its aim was to sow discord both within the US itself, but more especially within the Transatlantic alliance which was viewed as inimical to Russia's interests. Source C, a senior Russian financial official said the TRUMP operation should be seen in terms of PUTIN's desire to return to Nineteenth

Century 'Great Power' politics anchored upon countries' interests rather than the ideals-based international order established after World War Two. S/he had overheard PUTIN talking this way to close associates on several occasions.

2. In terms of specifics, Source A confided that the Kremlin had been feeding TRUMP and his team valuable intelligence on his opponents, including Democratic presidential candidate Hillary CLINTON, for several years [see more below]. This was confirmed by Source D close associate of TRUMP who had organized and managed his recent trips to Moscow, and who reported, also in June 2016, that this Russian intelligence had been "very helpful". The Kremlln's cultivation operation on TRUMP also had comprised offering him various lucrative real estate development

business deals in Russia, especially in relation to the ongoing 2018 World Cup soccer tournament. However, so far, for reasons unknown, TRUMP had not taken up any of these.

3. However, there were other aspects to TRUMP's engagement with the Russian authorities. One which had borne fruit for them was to exploit personal obsessions and sexual perversion in order to obtain suitable *'kompromat'* [compromising material] on him. According to Source D, when s/he had been present, TRUMP's (perverted) conduct in Moscow included hiring the presidential suite of the Ritz Carlton Hotel, where he knew President and Mrs. OBAMA [whom he hated] had stayed on one of their official trips to Russia, and defiling the bed where they had slept by employing a number of prostitutes to perform a 'golden showers' (urination) show in front of him. The hotel was known to be under FSE control with microphones and concealed cameras in all the main rooms to record anything they wanted to.

4. The Moscow Ritz Carlton episode involving TRUMP reported above was confirmed by Source E [redacted] who said that s/he and several of the staff were aware of it at the time and subsequently. S/he believed it had happened in 2013. Source E

provided an introduction for a company ethnic Russian operative to Source F, a female staffer at the hotel when TRUMP had stayed there, who also confirmed the story. Speaking separately in June 2016, Source B [the

former top level Russian intelligence officer] asserted that unorthodox behavior in Russia over the years had provided the authorities there with enough embarrassing material on the now

Republican presidential candidate to be able to blackmail him if they so wished

5. Asked about the Kremlin's reported intelligence feed to TRUMP over recent years and rumours about a Russian dossier of '*kornpromat*' on Hillary CLINTON (being circulated), Source B confirmed the file's existence. S/he confided in a trusted compatriot that it had been collated by Department of the FSB for many years, dating back to her husband Bill's presidency, and comprised mainly eavesdropped conversations of various sorts rather than details/evidence of unorthodox or embarrassing behavior. Some of the conversations were from bugged comments CLINTON had made on her various trips to Russia and focused on things on various things she had said which contradicted her current position on various issues. Others were most probably from phone intercepts.

6. Continuing on this theme, Source G, a senior Kremlin official, confided that the CLINTON dossier was controlled exclusively by chief Kremlin spokesman Dimitry PESKOV, who was responsible for compiling/handling it on the explicit instructions of PUTIN himself. The dossier however had not as yet been made available abroad, including to TRUMP or his campaign team. At present it was unclear what PUTIN's intentions were in that regard.

20 June 2016

Top of Form

## COMPANY INTELLIGENCE REPORT 2016/086

## CRIME: A SYNOPSIS OF RUSSIAN STATE SPONSORED AND

## OTHER CYBER OFFENSIVE (CRIMINAL) OPERATIONS

### CONFIDENTIAL/SENSITIVE SOURCE

Summary

- Russia has extensive programme of state-sponsored offensive cyber operations. External targets include foreign governments and big corporations, especially banks. FSB leads on cyber within Russian apparatus. Limited success in attacking top foreign targets like G7 governments, security services but much more on second tier ones through IT back doors, using corporate and other visitors to Russia

- FSB often uses coercion and blackmail to recruit most capable cyber operatives in Russia into its state-sponsored programmes. Heavy use also, both wittingly and unwittingly, of CIS emigres working in western corporations and ethnic Russians employed by neighbouring governments, e.g. Latvia

- Example cited of successful Russian cyber operation targeting senior Western business visitor. Provided back door into important Western institutions

- Example given of US citizen of Russian origin approached by FSB and offered incentive of "investment" in his business when visiting Moscow

- Problems however for Russian authorities themselves in countering local hackers and cyber criminals, operating outside state control. Central Bank claims there were over 20 serious attacks on correspondent accounts held by CBR in 2015, comprising Rubles several billion in fraud

- Some details given of leading non-state Russian cyber criminal groups

Details

1. Speaking in June 2016, a number of Russian figures with a detailed knowledge of national cyber crime, both state-sponsored and otherwise, outlined the current situation in this area. A former senior intelligence officer divided Russian state-sponsored offensive cyber operations into four categories (in order of priority): targeting foreign, especially western governments; penetrating leading foreign business corporations, especially banks; domestic monitoring of the elite; and attacking political opponents both at home and abroad. The former intelligence officer reported that the Federal Security Service (FSB) was the lead organization within the Russian state apparatus for cyber operations.

2. In terms of the success of Russian offensive cyber operations to date, a senior government figure reported that there had been only limited success in penetrating foreign targets. These comprised western (especially G7 and NATO) governments, security services and central banks, and the IFIs. To compensate for this shortfall massive effort had been invested, with much

greater success, in attacking the "secondary targets", particularly western private banks and the governments of smaller states allied to the West. S/he mentioned Latvia in this regard. Hundreds of agents, either consciously cooperating with the FSB or whose personal and professional IT systems had been unwittingly compromised, were recruited. Many were people who had ethnic and family ties to Russia and or had been incentivized financially to cooperate. Such people often would receive monetary inducements or contractual favours from the Russian state or its agents in return. This had created difficulties for parts of the Russian state apparatus in obliging/indulging them e.g. the Central Bank of Russia knowingly having to cover up for such agents' money laundering operations through the Russian financial system.

3. In terms of the FSB's recruitment of capable cyber operatives to carry out its, ideally deniable, offensive cyber operations, a Russian IT specialist with direct knowledge reported in June 2016 that this was often done using coercion and blackmail. In terms of 'foreign' agents, the FSB was

approaching US citizens of Russian (Jewish) origin on business trips to Russia. In one case a US citizen of Russian ethnicity had been visiting Moscow to attract investors in his new information technology program. The FSB clearly knew this and had offered to provide seed capital to this

person in return for them being able to access and modify his IP, with a view to targeting priority foreign targets by planting a Trojan virus in the software. The US visitor was told this was common practice. The FSB also had implied significant operational success as a result of installing cheap Russian IT games containing their own malware unwittingly by targets on their PCs and other platforms.

4. In a more advanced and successful FSB operation, an IT operator inside a leading Russian SOE, who previously had been employed on conventional (defensive) IT work there, had been under instruction for the last year to conduct an offensive cyber operation against a foreign director of the company. Although the latter was apparently an infrequent visitor to Russia, the FSB now successfully had penetrated his personal IT and through this had managed to access various important institutions in the West through the back door.

5. In terms of other technical IT platforms, an FSB cyber operative flagged up the 'Telegram' enciphered commercial system as having been of especial concern and therefore heavily targeted by the FSB, not least because it was used frequently by Russian internal political activists and

oppositionists. His/her understanding was that the FSB now successfully had cracked this communications software and therefore it was no longer secure to use.

6. The senior Russian government figure cited above also reported that non-state sponsored cyber crime was becoming an increasing problem inside Russia for the government and authorities there. The Central Bank of Russia claimed that in 2015 alone there had been more than 20 attempts at serious cyber embezzlement of money from corresponding accounts held there, comprising several billions Rubles. More generally, s/he understood there were circa 15 major organized crime groups in the country involved in cyber crime, all of which continued to operate largely outside state and FSB control. These included the so-called `Anunak', 'Buktrap' and `Metel' organizations.

26 July 2015

SENSITIVE SOURCE

COMPANY INTELLIGENCE REPORT 2016/095

PRESIDENTIAL ELECTION: FURTHER INDICATIONS OF

EXTENSIVE CONSPIRACY BETWEEN CAMPAIGN TEAM
AND THE KREMLIN

Summary

- Further evidence of extensive conspiracy between campaign team and Kremlin, sanctioned at highest levels and involving Russian diplomatic staff based in the US

- TRUMP associate admits Kremlin behind recent appearance of DNC e-mails on WikiLeaks, as means of maintaining plausible deniability

- Agreed exchange of information established in both directions. Team using moles within DNC and hackers in the US as well as outside in Russia. PUTIN motivated by fear and hatred of Hillary CLINTON. Russians receiving intel from team on Russian oligarchs and their families in US

- Mechanism for transmitting this intelligence involves "pension" disbursements to Russian emigres living in US as cover, using consular officials in New York, DC and Miami

- Suggestion from source close to TRUMP and MANAFORT
that Republican campaign team happy to have Russia as media
bogeyman to mask more extensive corrupt business ties to China
and other emerging countries

Detail

1. Speaking in confidence to a compatriot in late July 2016,
Source B, an ethnic Russian close associate of Republican US
presidential candidate Donald TRUMP, admitted that there was a
well-developed conspiracy of co-operation between them and the
Russian leadership. This was

managed on the TRUMP side by the Republican candidate's
campaign manager, Paul MANAFORT, who was using foreign
policy advisor, Carter PAGE, and others as intermediaries.
The two sides had a mutual interest in defeating Democratic
presidential candidate Hillary CLINTON, whom President
PUTIN apparently both hated and feared.

2. Inter alia, Source E, acknowledged that the Russian regime
had been behind the recent leak of embarrassing e-mail
messages, emanating from the Democratic National Committee
(DNC), to the WikiLeaks platform. The reason for using
WikiLeaks was "plausible deniability" and the

operation had been conducted with the full knowledge and
support of TRUMP and senior members of his campaign team.
In return the TRUMP team had agreed to sideline Russian
intervention in Ukraine as a campaign issue and to raise defence
commitments in the Baltics and Eastern Europe to deflect
attention away from Ukraine, a priority for PUTIN who needed

to cauterize the subject.

3. In the wider context campaign/Kremlin co-operation, Source E claimed that the intelligence network being used against CLINTON comprised three elements. There were agents/ facilitators within the Democratic Party structure itself; secondly Russian emigre and associated offensive cyber operators based in the and thirdly, state-sponsored cyber operatives working in Russia. All three elements had played an important role to date. On the mechanism for rewarding relevant assets based in the US, and effecting a two-way flow of intelligence and other useful information, Source claimed that Russian diplomatic staff in key cities such as New York, Washington DC and Miami were using the emigre "pension" distribution system as cover. The

operation therefore depended on key people in the US Russian émigré community for its success. Tens of thousands of dollars were involved.

4. In terms of the intelligence flow from the TRUMP team to Russia, Source reported that much of this concerned the activities of business oligarchs and their families' activities and assets in the US, with which PUTIN and the Kremlin seemed preoccupied.

5. Commenting on the negative media publicity surrounding alleged Russian interference in the US election campaign in support of TRUMP, Source said he understood that the Republican candidate and his team were relatively relaxed about this because it deflected media and the

Democrats' attention away from TRUMP's business dealings in China and other emerging markets. Unlike in Russia, these were substantial and involved the payment of large bribes and kickbacks which, were they to become public, would be potentially very damaging to their campaign.


6. Finally, regarding claimed minimal investment profile in Russia, a separate source with direct knowledge said this had not been for want of trying. Previous efforts had included exploring the real estate sector in St Petersburg as well as Moscow but in the end TRUMP had had to settle for the use of extensive sexual services there from local prostitutes rather than business success.

COMPANY INTELLIGENCE REPORT 2016/094

RUSSIA: SECRET KREMLIN MEETINGS ATTENDED BY TRUMP ADVISOR,

CARTER PAGE IN MOSCOW (JULY 2016)

Summary

-TRUMP advisor Carter PAGE holds secret meetings in Moscow with SECHIN and senior Kremlin Internal Affairs official, DIVYEKIN

-SECHIN raises issues of future bilateral US-Russia energy co-operation and associated lifting of western sanctions against Russia over Ukraine. PAGE non-committal in response

-DIVYEKIN discusses release of Russian dossier of "kompromat" on TRUMP's opponent, Hillary CLINTON, but also hints at Kremlin possession of such material on TRUMP

Detail

1. Speaking in July 2016, a Russian source close to Rosneft [Russian oil company] President, PUTIN close associate and US-sanctioned individual, Igor SECHIN, confided the details of a recent secret meeting between him and visiting Foreign Affairs

*Trumpocalypse Now!*

Advisor to Republican presidential candidate Donald TRUMP, Carter PAGE.

2.According to SECHIN's associate, the Rosneft President (CEO) had raised with PAGE the issues of future bilateral energy cooperation and prospects for an associated move to lift Ukraine-related western sanctions against Russia. PAGE had reacted positively to this demarche by SECHIN but had been generally non-committal in response.

3.Speaking separately, also in July 2016, an official close to Presidential Administration Head, S. IVANOV, confided in a compatriot that a senior colleague in the Internal Political Department of the PA, DIVYEKIN (nfd) also had met secretly with PAGE on his recent visit. Their agenda had included DIVYEKIN raising a dossier of "kompromat" the Kremlin possessed on Democratic presidential rival, Hillary CLINTON, and its possible release to the Republican's campaign team.

4.However, the Kremlin official close to S. added that s/ he believed DIVYEKIN also had hinted (or indicated more strongly) that the Russian leadership also had "kompromat" on TRUMP which the latter should bear in mind in his dealings with them.

19 July 2016

Top of Form

COMPANY INTELLIGENCE REPORT 2016/097

RUSSIA-US PRESIDENTIAL ELECTION: KREMLIN
CONCERN THAT POLITICAL FALLOUT FROM DNC
E-MAIL HACKING AFFAIR SPIRALLING OUT OF
CONTROL

Summary

-Kremlin concerned that political fallout from DNC e-mail
hacking operation is spiraling out of control. Extreme
nervousness among associates as result of negative media
attention/accusations

-Russians meanwhile keen to cool situation and maintain
"plausible deniability" of existing/ongoing operations. Therefore
unlikely to be any ratcheting up offensive plays in immediate
future

-Source close to TRUMP campaign however confirms regular
exchange with Kremlin has existed for at least 8 years, including
intelligence fed back to Russia on oligarchs' activities in US

-Russians apparently have promised not to use "kompromat"
they hold on TRUMP as leverage, given high levels of voluntary
co-operation forthcoming from his team

Detail

1. Speaking in confidence to a trusted associate in late July 2016, a Russian emigre figure close to the Republican US presidential candidate Donald campaign team commented on the fallout from publicity surrounding the Democratic National Committee (DNC) e-mail hacking scandal. The emigre said there was a high level of anxiety within the TRUMP team as a result of various accusations levelled against them and indications from the Kremlin that President PUTIN and others in the leadership thought things had gone too far now and risked spiraling out of control.

2. Continuing on this theme, the emigre associate of TRUMP opined that the Kremlin wanted the situation to calm but for "plausible deniability" to be maintained concerning its (extensive) and operations. S/he therefore judged that it was unlikely these would be ratcheted up, at least for the time being.

3. However, in terms of established operational liaison between the TRUMP team and the Kremlin, the emigre confirmed that an intelligence exchange had been running between them for at least 8 years. Within this context priority requirement had been for intelligence on the activities, business and otherwise, in the US of leading Russian oligarchs and their families. TRUMP and his associates duly had obtained and supplied the Kremlin with this information.

4. Finally, the emigre said s/he understood the Kremlin had more intelligence on CLINTON and her campaign but he did

not know the details or when or if it would be released. As far as "kompromat" (compromising information) on TRUMP were concerned, although there was plenty of this, he understood the Kremlin had given its word that it would not be deployed against the Republican presidential candidate given how helpful and co-operative his team had been over several years, and particularly of late.

30 July 2016

COMPANY INTELLIGENCE REPORT 2016/100

GROWING BACKLASH IN KREMLIN TO DNC HACKING
AND
TRUMP SUPPORT OPERATIONS

Summary

-Head of PA IVANOV laments Russian intervention in US presidential election and black PR against CLINTON and the DNC. Vows not to supply intelligence to Kremlin PR operatives again. Advocates now sitting tight and denying everything

-Presidential spokesman PESKOV the main protagonist in Kremlin campaign to aid TRUMP and damage CLINTON. He is now scared and fears being made scapegoat by leadership for backlash in US. Problem compounded by his botched intervention in recent Turkish crisis

-Premier MEDVEDEV's office furious over DNC hacking and associated anti-Russian publicity. Want good relations with US and ability to travel there. Refusing to support or help cover up after PESKOV

-Talk now in Kremlin regarding withdrawing from presidential race altogether, but this still largely wishful thinking by more liberal elements in Moscow

Detail

1. Speaking in early August 2016, two well-placed and established Kremlin sources outlined the divisions and backlash in Moscow arising from the leaking of Democratic National Committee (DNC) e-mails and the wider operation being conducted in the US. Head of Presidential

Administration, Sergei IVANOV, was angry at the recent turn of events. He believed the Kremlin "team" involved, led by presidential spokesman Dmitriy PESKOV, had gone too far in interfering in foreign affairs with their "elephant in a china shop." IVANOV claimed always to have opposed the handling and exploitation of intelligence by this PR "team".

Following the backlash against such foreign interference in US politics, IVANOV was advocating that the only sensible course of action now for the Russian leadership was to "sit tight and deny everything".

2. Continuing on this theme the source close to IVANOV reported that PESKOV now was "scared shitless" that he would be scapegoated by PUTIN and the Kremlin and held responsible for the backlash against Russian political interference in the US election. IVANOV was determined to stop PESKOV playing an independent role in relation to the US going forward and the source fully expected the presidential spokesman now to lay low. Position was not helped by a botched attempt by him also to interfere in the recent failed coup in Turkey from a government

relations (GR) perspective (no further details).

3. The extent of disquiet and division within Moscow caused by the backlash against Russian interference in the US election

was underlined by a second source, close to premier Dmitriy MEDVEDEV (DAM). S/he said the Russian prime minister and his colleagues wanted to have good relations with the US, regardless of who was in power there, and not least so as to be able to travel there in future, either officially or privately. They were openly refusing to cover up for PESKOV and others involved in the operations or to support his counter-attack of allegations

against the USG for its alleged hacking of the Russian government and state agencies.

4. According to the first source, close to IVANOV, there had been talk in the Kremlin of TRUMP being forced to withdraw from the presidential race altogether as a result of recent events, ostensibly on grounds of his statements and unsuitability for high office. This might not be so

bad for Russia in the circumstances but in the view of the source, it remained largely wishful thinking on the part of those in the regime opposed to PESKOV and his "botched" operations, at least for the time being.

5 August 2016

Top of Form

COMPANY INTELLIGENCE REPORT 2016/101

PRESIDENTIAL ELECTION: SENIOR KREMLIN FIGURE
OUTLINES EVOLVING RUSSIAN TACTICS IN PRO-
TRUMP, ANTI-CLINTON OPERATION

Summary

- Head of PA, IVANOV assesses Kremlin intervention in
US presidential election and outlines leadership thinking on
operational way forward

- No new leaks envisaged, as too politically risky, but rather
further exploitation of WikiLeaks material already disseminated
to exacerbate divisions

- Educated US youth to be targeted as a swing vote in attempt to
turn them over to TRUMP

- Russian leadership, including N, celebrating perceived success
to date in splitting US hawks and elite

- Kremlin engaging with several high profile US players,
including STEIN, PAGE and former DIA Director Michael
FLYNN and funding their recent visits to Moscow

Details


1. Speaking in confidence to a close colleague in early August 2016, Head of the Russian Presidential Administration (PA), Sergei IVANOV, assessed the impact and results of Kremlin intervention in the US presidential election to date. Although most commentators believed that the Kremlin was behind the leaked e-mails, this remained technically deniable. Therefore the Russians would not risk their position for the time being with new leaked material, even to a third party like WikiLeaks. Rather the tactics would be to spread rumours and misinformation about the content of what already had been leaked and make up new content.


2. Continuing on this theme, IVANOV said that the audience to be targeted by such operations was the educated youth in America as the PA assessed that there was still a chance they could be persuaded to vote for Republican candidate Donald TRUMP as a protest against the Washington establishment (in the form of Democratic candidate Hillary CLINTON). The hope was that even if she won, as a result of this CLINTON in power would be bogged down in working for internal reconciliation in the US, rather than being able to focus on foreign policy which would damage Russia's interests. This also should give President PUTIN more room for manoeuvre in the run-up to Russia's own presidential election in 2018.


3. IVANOV reported that although the Kremlin had underestimated the strength of US media and liberal reaction to the DNC hack and links to Russia, PUTIN was generally satisfied with the progress of the any operation to date. He

recently had had a drink with PUTIN to mark this. In his view, the US had tried to divide the Russian elite with sanctions but failed, whilst they, by contrast, had succeeded in splitting the US hawks inimical to Russia and the Washington elite more generally, half of whom had refused to endorse any presidential candidate as a result of Russian intervention.

4. Speaking separately, also in early August 2016, a Kremlin official involved in US relations commented on aspects of the Russian operation to date. Its goals have been threefold — US actors how Moscow could help them [?]; gathering relevant intelligence; and creating and disseminating compromising information "kompromat". This had involved the Kremlin supporting various US political figures, including funding indirectly their recent visits to Moscow. S/he named a delegation from Lyndon LAROUCHE; presidential candidate Jill STEIN of the Green Party; TRUMP foreign policy adviser Carter PAGE and former DIA Director Michael in this regard and as successful In terms of perceived outcomes.

10 August 2016

COMPANY INTELLIGENCE REPORT 2016/102


PRESIDENTIAL ELECTION: REACTION IN TRUMP CAMP
TO RECENT NEGATIVE PUBLICITY ABOUT RUSSIAN
INTERFERENCE AND LIKELY RESULTING TACTICS
GOING FORWARD

Summary


- TRUMP campaign insider reports recent DNC e-mail leaks
were aimed at switching SANDERS (protest) voters away from
CLINTON and over to TRUMP


-Admits Republican campaign underestimated resulting negative
reaction from US liberals, elite and media and forced to change
course as result


- Need now to turn tables on use of PUTIN as bogeyman in
election, although some resentment at Russian president's
perceived attempt to undermine US and system over and above
swinging presidential election

Detail

1. Speaking in confidence on 9 August 2016, an ethnic
Russian associate of Republican US presidential candidate
Donald TRUMP discussed the reaction inside his camp, and
revised tactics therein resulting from recent negative publicity
concerning Moscow's clandestine involvement in the campaign.
Associate reported that the aim of leaking the DNC e-mails to

WikiLeaks during the Democratic Convention had been to swing supporters of Bernie SANDERS away from Hillary CLINTON and across to TRUMP. These voters were perceived as activist and anti -status quo and anti–establishment and in that regard sharing many features with the TRUMP campaign, including a visceral dislike of Hillary CLINTON. This objective had been conceived and promoted, inter alia, foreign policy adviser Carter PAGE who had discussed it directly with the ethnic Russian associate.

2. Continuing on this theme, the ethnic Russian associate of TRUMP assessed that the problem was that the TRUMP campaign had underestimated the strength of the negative reaction from liberals and especially the conservative elite to Russian interference. This was forcing a rethink and a likely change of tactics. The main objective in the short term was to check Democratic candidate Hillary CLINTON's successful exploitation of the PUTIN as bogeyman/Russian interference story to tarnish TRUMP and bolster her own (patriotic) credentials. The TRUMP campaign was focusing on tapping into supporting the American television media to achieve this, as they reckoned this resource had been underused by them to date.

3. However, associate also admitted that there was a fair amount of anger and resentment within the Republican candidate's team at what was perceived by PUTIN as going beyond the objective of weakening CLINTON and bolstering TRUMP, by attempting to exploit the situation to undermine the US government and democratic system more generally. It was unclear at present how this aspect of the situation would play out in the weeks to come.

10 August 2016

COMPANY INTELLIGENCE REPORT 2016/136


PRESIDENTIAL ELECTION: FURTHER DETAILS OF
TRUMP LAWYER SECRET LIAISON WITH THE KREMLIN


Summary


- Kremlin insider reports TRUMP lawyer secret meeting/s with
Kremlin officials in August 2016 was/were held in Prague


- Russian parastatal organization Rossotrudnichestvo used as
cover for this liaison and premises

in Czech capital may have been used for the meeting/s


- Pro-PUTIN leading Duma figure, KOSACHEV, reportedly
involved as "plausibly deniable" facilitator and may have
participated in the August meeting with COHEN


Detail


1. Speaking to a compatriot and friend on 19 October 2016, a
Kremlin insider provided further details of reported clandestine
meeting/s between Republican presidential candidate Donald
TRUMP's lawyer Michael COHEN and Kremlin representative
in August 2016. Although the communication between them had
to be cryptic for security reasons, the Kremlin insider clearly

indicated to his/her friend that the reported contact/s took place in Prague, Czech Republic.

2. Continuing on this theme, the Kremlin insider highlighted the importance of the Russian

parastatal organisation, Rossotrudnichestvo, in this contact between TRUMP campaign

representative/s and Kremlin officials. Rossotrudnichestvo was being used as cover for this

relationship and its office in Prague may well have been used to host the COHEN Russian

Presidential Administration (PA) meeting/s. It was considered a "plausibly deniable" vehicle for this, whilst remaining entirely under Kremlin control.

3. The Kremlin insider went on to identify leading Duma figure, Konstantin KOSACHEV (Head of the Foreign Relations Committee) as an important figure in the TRUMP campaign-Kremlin liaison operation. KOSACHEV, also "plausibly deniable" being part of the Russian legislature rather than executive, had facilitated the contact in Prague and by implication, may have attended the meeting/s with COHEN there in August.

Company Comment

We reported previously, in our Company Intelligence Report 2016/135 of 19 October 2016 from the same source, that COHEN met officials from the PA Legal Department clandestinely in an EU country in August 2016. This was in order to clean up the mess left behind by western media

revelations of TRUMP ex-campaign manager MANAFORT's corrupt relationship with the former pro-Russian YANUKOVYCH regime in Ukraine and TRUMP foreign policy advisor, Carter secret meetings in Moscow with senior regime figures in July 2016. According to the Kremlin advisor, these meeting were originally scheduled for COHEN in Moscow but shifted to what was considered an operationally "soft" EU country when it was judged too compromising

for him to travel to the Russian capital.

20 October 2016

COMPANY INTELLIGENCE REPORT 2016/105

## RUSSIAN/UKRAINE: THE DEMISE 0F CAMPAIGN MANAGER PAUL MANAFORT

-Ex-Ukrainian President YANUKOVYCH confides directly to PUTIN that he authorized kick-back payments to MANAFORT, as alleged in western media. Assures Russian President however there is no documentary evidence/trail

-PUTIN and Russian leadership remain worried however and skeptical that YANUKOVYCH has fully covered the traces of these payments to former campaign manager

-Close associate explains reasoning behind recent resignation. Ukraine revelations played part but others wanted MANAFORT out for various reasons, especially LEWANDOWSKI who remains influential

Detail

1. Speaking in late August 2016, in the immediate aftermath of Paul MANAFORT's resignation as campaign manager for US Republican presidential candidate Donald TRUMP, a well-placed Russian figure reported on a recent meeting between President PUTIN and ex-President YANUKOVYCH of Ukraine. This had been held in secret on 15 August near Volgograd, Russia and the western media revelations about MANAFORT and Ukraine

had featured prominently on the agenda. YANUKOVYCH had confided in PUTIN that he did authorise and order substantial kick-back payments to MANAFORT as alleged but sought to reassure him that there was no documentary trail left behind which could provide clear evidence of this.

2. Given YANUKOVICH's (unimpressive) record in covering up his own corrupt tracks in the past, PUTIN and others in the Russian leadership were skeptical about the ex-Ukrainian president's reassurances on this as relating to MANAFORT. They therefore still feared the scandal had legs, especially as MANAFORT had been commercially active in Ukraine right

up to the time (in March 2016) when he joined campaign team. For them it therefore remained a point of potential political vulnerability and embarrassment.

Bottom of Form

3. Speaking separately, also in late August 2016, an American political figure associated with Donald TRUMP and his campaign outlined the reasons behind MANAFORT's recent demise. S/he said it was true that the Ukraine corruption revelations had played a part in this but also,

several senior players close to TRUMP had wanted MANAFORT out primarily to loosen his control on strategy and policy formulation. Of particular importance in this regard was predecessor as campaign manager, Corey LEWANDOWSKI, who hated MANAFORT

personally and remained close to TRUMP with whom he discussed the presidential campaign on a regular basis.

22 August 2016

COMPANY INTELLIGENCE REPORT 2016/111

## KREMLIN FALLOUT FROM MEDIA EXPOSURE OF INTERFERENCE IN THE US PRESIDENTIAL CAMPAIGN

Summary

-Kremlin orders senior staff to remain silent in media and private on allegations of Russian interference in US presidential campaign

- Senior figure however confirms gist of allegations and reports IVANOV sacked as Head of Administration on account of giving PUTIN poor advice on issue. VAINO selected as his replacement partly because he was not involved in operation/s

-Russians do have further "kompromat" on CLINTON (e-mails) and considering disseminating it after Duma (legislative elections) in late September. Presidential spokesman PESKOV continues to lead on this

- However, equally important is Kremlin objective to shift policy consensus favorably to Russia in US whoever wins. Both presidential candidates' opposition to TPP and TTIP viewed as a result in this respect

- Senior Russian diplomat withdrawn from Washington embassy

on account of potential exposure in US presidential election
operation /s


Detail


1. Speaking in confidence to a trusted compatriot in mid-
September 2016, a senior member of the Russian Presidential
Administration (PA) commented on the political fallout from
recent western media revelations about Moscow's intervention,
in favor of Donald TRUMP and against Hillary CLINTON, in
the US presidential election. The PA official reported that the
issue had become incredibly sensitive and that President PUTIN
had issued direct orders that Kremlin and government insiders
should not discuss it in public or even in private.


2. Despite this, the PA official confirmed, from direct knowledge,
that the gist of the allegations was true. PUTIN had been
receiving conflicting advice on interfering from three separate
and expert groups. On one side had been the Russian ambassador
to the US, Sergei KISLYAK and the Ministry of Foreign
Affairs, together with an independent and informal network
run by presidential foreign policy advisor, Yuri USHAKOV
(KISLYAK's predecessor in Washington) who had urged caution
and the potential negative impact on Russia from the operation/s.
On the other side was former PA Head, Sergei IVANOV, backed
by Russian Foreign Intelligence (SVR), who had advised PUTIN
that the anti- CLINTON operation/s would be both effective and
plausibly deniable with little blowback. The first group/s had
been proven right and this had

been the catalyst in PUTIN's decision to sack IVANOV
(unexpectedly) as PA Head in August. His successor, Anton
VAINO, had been selected for the job partly because he had not

been involved in the US presidential election operation/s.

3. Continuing on this theme, the senior PA official said the situation now was that the Kremlin had further "kompromat" on candidate CLINTON and had been considering releasing this via "plausibly deniable" channels after the Duma (legislative) elections were out of the way in mid-

September. There was however a growing train of thought and associated lobby, arguing that the Russians could still make candidate CLINTON look "weak and stupid" by provoking her into railing against PUTIN and Russia without the need to release more of her e-mails. Presidential

Spokesman, Dmitriy PESKOV remained a key figure in the operation, although any final decision on dissemination of further material would be taken by PUTIN himself.

4. The senior PA official also reported that a growing element in Moscow's intervention in the US presidential election campaign was the objective of shifting the US political consensus in Russia's perceived interests regardless of who won. It basically comprised of pushing candidate

CLINTON away from President policies. The best example of this was that both candidates now openly opposed the draft trade agreements, TPP and TTIP, which were assessed by Moscow as

detrimental to Russian interests. Other issues where the Kremlin was looking to shift the US policy consensus were Ukraine and Syria. Overall however, the presidential election was considered still to be too close to call.

5. Finally, speaking separately to the same compatriot, a senior Russian MFA official reported that as a prophylactic measure,

a leading Russian diplomat, Mikhail KULAGIN, had been withdrawn from Washington at short notice because Moscow feared his heavy involvement in the US presidential election operation, including the so-called veterans pensions ruse (reported previously), would be exposed in the media there. His replacement, Andrei BONDAREV however was clean in this regard.

Company Comment

The substance of what was reported by the senior Russian PA official in paras 1 and 2 above, including the reasons for Sergei dismissal, was corroborated independently by a former top level Russian intelligence officer and Kremlin insider, also in mid-September.

14 September 2016

COMPANY INTELLIGENCE REPORT 2016/112

## PRESIDENTIAL ELECTION: KREMLIN-ALPHA GROUP CO-OPERATION

Summary

-Top level Russian official confirms current closeness of Alpha Group-PUTIN relationship. Significant favors continue to be done in both directions and FRIDMAN and AVEN still giving informal advice to PUTIN, especially on the US

- Key intermediary in relationship identified as Oleg GOVORUN, currently Head Of a Presidential Administration department but throughout the 1990s, the Alpha executive who delivered illicit cash directly to PUTIN

-PUTIN personally unbothered about Alpha's current lack Of investment in Russia but under pressure from colleagues over this and able to exploit it as lever over Alpha interlocutors

Detail

1. Speaking to a trusted compatriot in mid-September 2016, a top level Russian government official commented on the history and current state of relations between President PUTIN and the Alpha Group Of businesses led by oligarchs Mikhail FRIDMAN, Petr AVEN and German KHAN. The Russian government figure reported that although they had had their ups and downs, the leading figures in Alpha currently were on very good terms with PUTIN. Significant favours continued to be done in both directions, primarily political ones for PUTIN and business/ legal ones for Alpha. Also, RIDMAN and AVEN continued to give informal advice to PUTIN on foreign policy, and especially

about the US where he distrusted advice being given to him by
officials.

 2. Although FRIDMAN recently had met directly with PUTIN
in Russia, much of the dialogue and business between them was
mediated through a senior Presidential Administration Official,
Oleg GOVORUN, who currently headed the department therein
responsible for Social Co-operation with the CIS. GOVORUN
was trusted by PUTIN and recently had accompanied
him to Uzbekistan to pay respects at the tomb of former president
KARIMOV. However according to the top level Russian
government official, during the 1990s GOVORUN had been
Head of Government Relations at Alpha Group and in reality, the
"driver" and "bag carrier" used
by FRIDMAN and AVEN to deliver large amounts of illicit
cash to the Russian president, at that time deputy Mayor of
St Petersburg. Given that and the continuing sensitivity of the
relationship, and need for plausible deniability, much of the
contact between them was now
indirect and entrusted to the relatively low profile GOVORUN.

3. The top level Russian government official described the
PUTIN-Alpha relationship as both carrot and stick. Alpha held
"kompromat" on PUTIN and his corrupt business activities from
the 1990s whilst although not personally overly bothered by
Alpha's failure to reinvest the proceeds of its TNK oil company
sale into the Russian economy. Since, the president was able to
use pressure on this count from senior Kremlin colleagues as a
lever on FRIDMAN and AVEN to make them do his political
bidding.

14 September 2016

COMPANY INTELLIGENCE REPORT 2016/113

## PRESIDENTIAL ELECTION- REPUBLICAN CANDIDATE TRUMP'S PRIOR ACTIVITIES IN ST PETERSBURG

Summary

- Two knowledgeable St Petersburg sources claim Republican candidate TRUMP has paid bribes and engaged in sexual activities there but key witnesses silenced and evidence hard to obtain

- Both believe Azeri business associate of TRUMP, Araz AGALAROV, will know the details

Detail

1. Speaking to a trusted compatriot in September 2016, two well-placed sources based in St Petersburg, one in the political/ business elite and the other involved in the local services and tourist industry, commented on Republican US presidential candidate Donald TRUMP's prior activities in the city.

2. Both knew TRUMP had visited St Petersburg on several occasions in the past and had been interested in doing business deals there involving real estate. The local business/political elite figure reported that TRUMP had paid bribes there to further

his interests but very discreetly and only through affiliated companies, making it very hard to prove. The local services industry source reported that TRUMP had participated in sex parties in the city too, but that all direct witnesses to this recently had been "silenced" i.e. bribed or coerced to disappear.

3. The two St Petersburg figures cited believed an Azeri business figure, Araz AGALAROV (with offices in Baku and London) had been closely involved with TRUMP in Russia and would know most of the details of what the Republican presidential candidate had got up to there.

14 September 2016

COMPANY INTELLIGENCE REPORT 2016/130

RUSSIA: KREMLIN ASSESSMENT OF TRUMP AND
RUSSIAN INTERFERENCE IN US PRESIDENTIAL
ELECTION

Summary

-Buyer's remorse sets in with Kremlin over TRUMP support
operation in US presidential election. Russian leadership
disappointed that leaked e-malls on CLINTON have not had
greater impact in campaign

-Russians have injected further material into the plausibly
deniable leaks pipeline which will continue to surface, but best
material already in public domain

-PUTIN angry with senior officials who "over-promised" on
TRUMP and further heads likely to

roll as result. Foreign Minister LAVROV may be next

-TRUMP supported by Kremlin because seen as divisive. anti-
establishment candidate who

would shake up current International status quo in Russia's favor.
Lead on TRUMP operation moved from Foreign Ministry to FSB
and then to presidential administration where it now sits

Detail

1. Speaking separately in confidence to a trusted compatriot in early October 2016, a senior Russian leadership figure and a Foreign Ministry official reported on recent developments

concerning the Kremlin's operation to support Republican candidate Donald TRUMP in the

US presidential election. The senior leadership figure said that a degree of buyer's remorse

was setting in among Russian leaders concerning TRUMP. PUTIN and his colleagues were

surprised and disappointed that leaks of Democratic candidate Hillary CLINTON's hacked

e-mails had not had greater impact on the campaign.

2. Continuing on this theme, the senior leadership figure commented that a stream of further

hacked CLINTON material already had been injected by the Kremlin into compliant western

media outlets like WikiLeaks which remained at least 'plausibly deniable', so the stream of

these would continue through October and up to the election. However s/he understood that

the best material the Russians had already was out and there were no real game-changers to come.

3. The Russian Foreign Ministry official, who had direct access to the TRUMP support

operation, reported that PUTIN was angry at his subordinate's "over-promising" on the

Republican presidential candidate, both in terms of his chances and reliability and being

able to cover and/or contain the US backlash over Kremlin interference. More heads

therefore were likely to roll, with the MFA the easiest target. Ironically, despite his consistent

urging of caution on the issue, Foreign Minister LAVROV could be the next one to go.


4. Asked to explain why PUTIN and the Kremlin had launched such an aggressive TRUMP support operation in the first place, the MFA official said that Russia needed to meet the liberal interactional status quo, including on Ukraine-related sanctions, which was seriously disadvantaging the country. TRUMP was viewed as divisive in disrupting the whole US

political system; anti-Establishment; and a pragmatist with whom they could do business. As

the TRUMP support operation had gained momentum, control of it had passed from the MFA

to the FSA and then into the presidential administration where it remained, a reflection of its growing significance over time. There was still a view in the Kremlin that TRUMP would

continue as a (divisive) political force even if he lost the presidency and may run for and be elected to another public office.


12 October 2016

COMPANY INTELLIGENCE REPORT 2016/133


PRESIDENTIAL ELECTION: FURTHER DETAILS OF
KREMLIN LIAISON WITH TRUMP CAMPAIGN


Summary


 - Close associate of SECHIN confirms his secret meeting in
Moscow with Carter PAGE in July


- Substance included offer (of large stake in Rosneft in return
for lifting of Russia sanctions. PAGE confirms this is TRUMP's
intention


- SECHIN continued to think TRUMP could win presidency up
to 7 October. Now looking to

reoriented his engagement with the US


- Kremlin insider highlights importance of lawyer, Michael
COHEN in covert relationship with Russia. COHEN's wife is of
Russian descent and her father a leading property developer in
Moscow


Detail

1. Speaking to a trusted compatriot in mid October 2016, a close associate of Rosneft President

and PUTIN ally Igor SECHIN elaborated on the reported secret meeting between the latter

and Carter PAGE, of US Republican presidential candidate's foreign policy team, in Moscow in

July 2016. The secret had been confirmed to him/her by a senior member of staff, in addition to by the Rbsneft President himself. It took place on either 7 or 8 July, the same day or the one after Carter PAGE made a public speech to the Higher Economic School in Moscow.

2. In terms of the substance of their discussion SECHIN's associate said that the Rosneft President was so keen to lift personal and corporate western sanctions imposed on the company, that he offered PAGE associates the brokerage of up to a 19 per cent (privatised) stake in Rosneft in return. PAGE had expressed interest and confirmed that were TRUMP elected US President, then sanctions on Russia would be lifted.

3. According to SECHIN's close associate, the Rosneft President had continued to believe that

TRUMP could win the US presidency right up to I7 October, when he assessed this was no

longer possible. SECHIN was keen to readapt accordingly and put feelers out to other business and political contacts in the US instead.

4. Speaking separately to the same compatriot in mid-October 2016, a Kremlin insider with direct access to the leadership

confirmed that a key role in the select TRUMP campaign/ Kremlin

relationship was being played by the Republican candidate's personal lawyer Michael COHEN.

[redacted]

Source comment

5. SECHIN's associate opined that although PAGE had not stated it explicitly to SECHN, he had clearly implied that in terms of his comment on TRUMP's intention to lift Russian sanctions if elected president, he was speaking with the Republican candidate's authority.

Company Comment

6. [redacted]

15 October 2016

COMPANY INTELLIGENCE REPORT 2016/135

PRESIDENTIAL ELECTION: THE IMPORTANT ROLE OF
TRUMP LAWYER COHEN IN SECRET LIAISON WITH THE
KREMLIN

Summary

- Kremlin insider outlines important role played by lawyer
COHEN in secret liaison with Russian leadership

- COHEN engaged with Russians in trying to cover up scandal of
MANAFORT and exposure of PAGE and meets Kremlin officials
secretly in the EU in August in pursuit of this goal

- These secret contacts continue but are now farmed out to
trusted agents in Kremlin linked institutes so as to remain
"plausibly deniable" for Russian regime

- Further confirmation that sacking of IVANOV and
appointments of VAINO and KIRIYENKO linked to need to
cover up Kremlin's TRUMP support operation

Detail

1. Speaking in confidence to a longstanding compatriot friend in

mid-October 2016, a Kremlin insider highlighted the importance of Republican presidential candidate Donald TRUMP's lawyer, Michael COHEN, in the ongoing secret liaison relationship between the New York

tycoon's campaign and the Russian leadership. COHEN's role had grown following the departure of Paul MANAFORT as campaign manager in August 2016. Prior to that MANAFORT had led for the TRUMP side.

2. According to the Kremlin insider, COHEN now was heavily engaged in a cover up and damage limitation operation in the attempt to prevent the full details of TRUMP's relationship with Russia being exposed. In pursuit of this aim, COHEN had met secretly with several Russian Presidential Administration (PA) Legal Department officials in an EU country in August 2016. The immediate issues had been to contain further scandals involving MANAFORT's commercial and political role in Russia/Ukraine and to limit the damage arising from exposure of

former TRUMP foreign policy advisor, Carter PAGE's secret meetings with Russian leadership figures in Moscow the previous month. The overall objective had been to "to sweep it all under the carpet and make sure no connections could be fully established or proven".

3. Things had become even "hotter" since August on the track. According to the Kremlin insider, this had meant that direct contact between the TRUMP team and Russia had been farmed out by the Kremlin to trusted agents of influence working in pro-government policy institutes like that of Law and Comparative Jurisprudence. COHEN however continued to lead for the TRUMP team.

4. Referring back to the (surprise) sacking of Sergei IVANOV as Head of PA in August 2016, his replacement by Anton VAINO and the appointment of former Russian premier Sergei KIRIYENKO to another senior position in the PA, the Kremlin insider repeated that this had been directly connected to the TRUMP support operation and the need to cover up now that it was being exposed by the USO and in the western media.

Company Comment

The Kremlin insider was unsure of the identities of the PA officials with whom COHEN met secretly in August, or the exact date/s and locations of the meeting/s. There were significant internal security barriers being erected in the PA as the TRUMP issue became more controversial and damaging. However s/he continued to try to obtain these.

19 October 2016

COMPANY INTELLIGENCE REPORT 2016/166

US/RUSSIA: FURTHER DETAILS OF SECRET DIALOGUE BETWEEN TRUMP

CAMPAIGN TEAM, KREMLIN AND ASSOCIATED HACKERS IN PRAGUE

Summary

- TRUMP's representative COHEN accompanied to Prague in August/September 2016 by 3 colleagues for secret discussions with Kremlin representatives and associated operators/hackers

- Agenda included how to process deniable cash payments to operatives; contingency plans for covering up operations; and action in event of an election victory

- Some further details of Russian representatives/operatives involved; Romanian hackers employed; and use of Bulgaria as bolt hole to "lie low"

- Anti-CLINTON hackers and other operatives paid by both TRUMP team and Kremlin, but with ultimate loyalty to Head of PA, and his successor/s

Detail

1. We reported previously (2016/135 and /136) on secret meeting/s held in Prague, Czech Republic in August 2016 between then Republican presidential candidate Donald TRUMP's representative, Michael COHEN and his interlocutors from the Kremlin working under cover of Russian Rossotrudnichestvo

2. [redacted] provided further details of these meeting/s and associated anti CLINTON/Democratic Party operations. COHEN had been accompanied to Prague by 3 colleagues and the timing of the visit was either in the last week of August or the first week of September. One of their main Russian interlocutors was Oleg SOLODUKHIN operating under Rossotrudnichestvo cover. According to the agenda comprised questions on how deniable cash payments were to be made to hackers who had worked in Europe under Kremlin direction against the CLINTON campaign and various contingencies for covering up these operations and Moscow's secret liaison with the TRUMP team more generally.

3. [redacted] reported that over the period March-September 2016 a company called [redacted] and its affiliates had been using botnets and porn traffic to transmit viruses, plant bugs, steal data and conduct "altering operations" against the Democratic Party leadership. Entities linked to one [redacted] were involved and he and another hacking expert both recruited under duress by the FSB [redacted] were significant players in this operation. In Prague, COHEN agreed to contingency plans for various scenarios to protect the operation, but it was to be done in the event that Hillary CLINTON won the presidency. It was important in this event that all cash payments owed were made quickly and discreetly and that cyber and other operators Paul MANAFORT and Carter PAGE in the secret TRUMP-

Kremlin liaison had been exposed in the media in the run-up to Prague and that damage limitation also was discussed by COHEN with the Kremlin representatives.

4. In terms of practical measures to be taken, it was agreed by the two sides in Prague to stand down various "Romanian hackers" (presumably based in their homeland or neighboring eastern Europe) and that other operatives should head for a bolt-hole in Plovdiv, Bulgaria where they should "lay low" on payments. IVANOV's associate said that the operatives involved had been paid by both TRUMP team and the Kremlin, though their orders and ultimate loyalty lay with IVANOV, as Head of the PA and thus ultimately responsible for the operation, and his designated successor/s after he was dismissed by president PUTIN in connection with the anti-CLINTON operation in mid August.

13 December 2016

(END OF THE DOSSIER)

The beast was given a mouth to utter proud words and blasphemies and to exercise its authority for forty-two months. It opened its mouth to blaspheme God, and to slander his name and his dwelling place and those who live in heaven. It was given power to wage war against God's holy people and to conquer them. And it was given authority over every tribe, people, language and nation. All inhabitants of the earth will worship the beast—all whose names have not been written in the Lamb's book of life, the Lamb who was slain from the creation of the world.
—Revelations 13:5-8

The Trump spectacle in the New York press, prior to election—growing the culture of ridicule later exemplified by Trump as the target of late night television comedians. It reflected Trump's attraction as spectacle and gained great ratings for these shows as well as the news shows. Trump's political power, however, came as a surprise.

The *National Enquirer* reports that Trump caught and fired Russian spy Michael Flynn. Shortly after this appeared, the *Wall Street Journal* reported that Flynn was ready to testify before the Senate Intelligence committee investigating Trump's Russian ties.

"I remember when <u>I</u> was the Donald!"

# Get these fascinating books from your nearest bookstore or directly from:
## Adventures Unlimited Press
### www.adventuresunlimitedpress.com

## COVERT WARS AND BREAKAWAY CIVILIZATIONS
### By Joseph P. Farrell

Farrell delves into the creation of breakaway civilizations by the Nazis in South America and other parts of the world. He discusses the advanced technology that they took with them at the end of the war and the psychological war that they waged for decades on America and NATO. He investigates the secret space programs currently sponsored by the breakaway civilizations and the current militaries in control of planet Earth. Plenty of astounding accounts, documents and speculation on the incredible alternative history of hidden conflicts and secret space programs that began when World War II officially "ended."

**292 Pages. 6x9 Paperback. Illustrated. $19.95. Code: BCCW**

## THE ENIGMA OF CRANIAL DEFORMATION
### Elongated Skulls of the Ancients
### By David Hatcher Childress and Brien Foerster

In a book filled with over a hundred astonishing photos and a color photo section, Childress and Foerster take us to Peru, Bolivia, Egypt, Malta, China, Mexico and other places in search of strange elongated skulls and other cranial deformation. The puzzle of why diverse ancient people—even on remote Pacific Islands—would use head-binding to create elongated heads is mystifying. Where did they even get this idea? Did some people naturally look this way—with long narrow heads? Were they some alien race? Were they an elite race that roamed the entire planet? Why do anthropologists rarely talk about cranial deformation and know so little about it? Color Section.

**250 Pages. 6x9 Paperback. Illustrated. $19.95. Code: ECD**

## ARK OF GOD
### The Incredible Power of the Ark of the Covenant
### By David Hatcher Childress

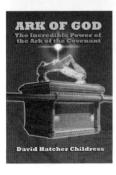

Childress takes us on an incredible journey in search of the truth about (and science behind) the fantastic biblical artifact known as the Ark of the Covenant. This object made by Moses at Mount Sinai—part wooden-metal box and part golden statue—had the power to create "lightning" to kill people, and also to fly and lead people through the wilderness. The Ark of the Covenant suddenly disappears from the Bible record and what happened to it is not mentioned. Was it hidden in the underground passages of King Solomon's temple and later discovered by the Knights Templar? Was it taken through Egypt to Ethiopia as many Coptic Christians believe? Childress looks into hidden history, astonishing ancient technology, and a 3,000-year-old mystery that continues to fascinate millions of people today. Color section.

**420 Pages. 6x9 Paperback. Illustrated. $22.00 Code: AOG**

## HIDDEN FINANCE, ROGUE NETWORKS & SECRET SORCERY
### The Fascist International, 9/11, & Penetrated Operations
### By Joseph P. Farrell
Pursuing his investigations of high financial fraud, international banking, hidden systems of finance, black budgets and breakaway civilizations, Farrell investigates the theory that there were not *two* levels to the 9/11 event, but *three*. He says that the twin towers were downed by the force of an exotic energy weapon, one similar to the Tesla energy weapon suggested by Dr. Judy Wood, and ties together the tangled web of missing money, secret technology and involvement of portions of the Saudi royal family. Farrell unravels the many layers behind the 9-11 attack, layers that include the Deutschebank, the Bush family, the German industrialist Carl Duisberg, Saudi Arabian princes and the energy weapons developed by Tesla before WWII.
**296 Pages. 6x9 Paperback. Illustrated. $19.95. Code: HFRN**

## THRICE GREAT HERMETICA AND THE JANUS AGE
### By Joseph P. Farrell
What do the Fourth Crusade, the exploration of the New World, secret excavations of the Holy Land, and the pontificate of Innocent the Third all have in common? Answer: Venice and the Templars. What do they have in common with Jesus, Gottfried Leibniz, Sir Isaac Newton, Rene Descartes, and the Earl of Oxford? Answer: Egypt and a body of doctrine known as Hermeticism. The hidden role of Venice and Hermeticism reached far and wide, into the plays of Shakespeare (a.k.a. Edward DeVere, Earl of Oxford), into the quest of the three great mathematicians of the Early Enlightenment for a lost form of analysis, and back into the end of the classical era, to little known Egyptian influences at work during the time of Jesus.
**354 Pages. 6x9 Paperback. Illustrated. $19.95. Code: TGHJ**

## THE THIRD WAY
### The Nazi International, European Union, & Corporate Fascism
### By Joseph P. Farrell
Pursuing his investigations of high financial fraud, international banking, hidden systems of finance, black budgets and breakaway civilizations, Farrell continues his examination of the post-war Nazi International, an "extra-territorial state" without borders or capitals, a network of terrorists, drug runners, and people in the very heights of financial power willing to commit financial fraud in amounts totaling trillions of dollars. Breakaway civilizations, black budgets, secret technology, occult rituals, international terrorism, giant corporate cartels, patent law and the hijacking of nature: Farrell explores 'the business model' of the post-war Axis elite.
**364 Pages. 6x9 Paperback. Illustrated. $19.95. Code: TTW**

## THE FREE-ENERGY DEVICE HANDBOOK
### A Compilation of Patents and Reports
### by David Hatcher Childress
A large-format compilation of various patents, papers, descriptions and diagrams concerning free-energy devices and systems. *The Free-Energy Device Handbook* is a visual tool for experimenters and researchers into magnetic motors and other "over-unity" devices. With chapters on the Adams Motor, the Hans Coler Generator, cold fusion, superconductors, "N" machines, space-energy generators, Nikola Tesla, T. Townsend Brown, and the latest in free-energy devices. Packed with photos, technical diagrams, patents and fascinating information, this book belongs on every science shelf.
**292 PAGES. 8X10 PAPERBACK. ILLUSTRATED. $16.95. CODE: FEH**

## TRUMPOCALYPSE NOW!
### The Triumph of the Conspiracy Spectacle
### by Kenn Thomas

*Trumpocalypse Now!* takes a look at Trump's career as a conspiracy theory celebrity, his trafficking in such notions as birtherism, Islamofascism and 9/11, the conspiracies of the Clinton era, and the JFK assassination. It also examines the controversies of the 2016 election, including the cyber-hacking of the DNC, the Russian involvement and voter fraud. Learn the parapolitcal realities behind the partisan divide and the real ideological underpinnings behind the country's most controversial president. Chapters include: Introduction: Alternative Facts; Conspiracy Celebrity–Trump's TV Career; Birtherism; 9/11 and Islamofascism; Clinton Conspiracies; JFK–Pro-Castro Fakery; Cyber Hacking the DNC; The Russian Connection; Votescam; Conclusion: Alternative Theories; more.
**6x9 Paperback. 380 Pages. Illustrated. $16.95. Code: TRPN**

## MIND CONTROL, OSWALD & JFK
### Introduction by Kenn Thomas

In 1969 the strange book *Were We Controlled?* was published which maintained that Lee Harvey Oswald was a special agent who was also a Mind Control subject who had received an implant in 1960. Thomas examines the evidence that Oswald had been an early recipient of the Mind Control implant technology and this startling role in the JFK Assassination. Also: the RHIC-EDOM Mind Control aspects concerning the RFK assassination and the history of implant technology.
**256 Pages. 6x9 Paperback. Illustrated. $16.00. Code: MCOJ**

## INSIDE THE GEMSTONE FILE
### Howard Hughes, Onassis & JFK
### By Kenn Thomas & David Childress

Here is the low-down on the most famous underground document ever circulated. Photocopied and distributed for over 20 years, the Gemstone File is the story of Bruce Roberts, the inventor of the synthetic ruby widely used in laser technology today, and his relationship with the Howard Hughes Company and ultimately with Aristotle Onassis, the Mafia, and the CIA. Hughes kidnapped and held a drugged-up prisoner for 10 years; Onassis and his role in the Kennedy Assassination; how the Mafia ran corporate America in the 1960s; more.
**320 Pages. 6x9 Paperback. Illustrated. $16.00. Code: IGF**

## ADVENTURES OF A HASHISH SMUGGLER
### by Henri de Monfreid

Nobleman, writer, adventurer and inspiration for the swashbuckling gun runner in the *Adventures of Tintin*, Henri de Monfreid lived by his own account "a rich, restless, magnificent life" as one of the great travelers of his or any age. The son of a French artist who knew Paul Gaugin as a child, de Monfreid sought his fortune by becoming a collector and merchant of the fabled Persian Gulf pearls. He was then drawn into the shadowy world of arms trading, slavery, smuggling and drugs. Infamous as well as famous, his name is inextricably linked to the Red Sea and the raffish ports between Suez and Aden in the early years of the twentieth century. De Monfreid (1879 to 1974) had a long life of many adventures around the Horn of Africa where he dodged pirates as well as the authorities.
**284 Pages. 6x9 Paperback. $16.95. Illustrated. Code AHS**

## TECHNOLOGY OF THE GODS
### The Incredible Sciences of the Ancients
### by David Hatcher Childress

Childress looks at the technology that was allegedly used in Atlantis and the theory that the Great Pyramid of Egypt was originally a gigantic power station. He examines tales of ancient flight and the technology that it involved; how the ancients used electricity; megalithic building techniques; the use of crystal lenses and the fire from the gods; evidence of various high tech weapons in the past, including atomic weapons; ancient metallurgy and heavy machinery; the role of modern inventors such as Nikola Tesla in bringing ancient technology back into modern use; impossible artifacts; and more.

**356 pages. 6x9 Paperback. Illustrated. $16.95. code: TGOD**

## THE ANTI-GRAVITY HANDBOOK
### edited by David Hatcher Childress

The new expanded compilation of material on Anti-Gravity, Free Energy, Flying Saucer Propulsion, UFOs, Suppressed Technology, NASA Cover-ups and more. Highly illustrated with patents, technical illustrations and photos. This revised and expanded edition has more material, including photos of Area 51, Nevada, the government's secret testing facility. This classic on weird science is back in a new format!

**230 PAGES. 7x10 PAPERBACK. ILLUSTRATED. $16.95. CODE: AGH**

## ANTI–GRAVITY & THE WORLD GRID

Is the earth surrounded by an intricate electromagnetic grid network offering free energy? This compilation of material on ley lines and world power points contains chapters on the geography, mathematics, and light harmonics of the earth grid. Learn the purpose of ley lines and ancient megalithic structures located on the grid. Discover how the grid made the Philadelphia Experiment possible. Explore the Coral Castle and many other mysteries, including acoustic levitation, Tesla Shields and scalar wave weaponry. Browse through the section on anti-gravity patents, and research resources.

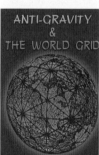

**274 PAGES. 7x10 PAPERBACK. ILLUSTRATED. $14.95. CODE: AGW**

## ANTI–GRAVITY & THE UNIFIED FIELD
### edited by David Hatcher Childress

Is Einstein's Unified Field Theory the answer to all of our energy problems? Explored in this compilation of material is how gravity, electricity and magnetism manifest from a unified field around us. Why artificial gravity is possible; secrets of UFO propulsion; free energy; Nikola Tesla and anti-gravity airships of the 20s and 30s; flying saucers as superconducting whirls of plasma; anti-mass generators; vortex propulsion; suppressed technology; government cover-ups; gravitational pulse drive; spacecraft & more.

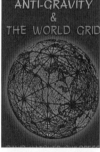

**240 PAGES. 7x10 PAPERBACK. ILLUSTRATED. $14.95. CODE: AGU**

## THE TIME TRAVEL HANDBOOK
### A Manual of Practical Teleportation & Time Travel
### edited by David Hatcher Childress

*The Time Travel Handbook* takes the reader beyond the government experiments and deep into the uncharted territory of early time travellers such as Nikola Tesla and Guglielmo Marconi and their alleged time travel experiments, as well as the Wilson Brothers of EMI and their connection to the Philadelphia Experiment—the U.S. Navy's forays into invisibility, time travel, and teleportation. Childress looks into the claims of time travelling individuals, and investigates the unusual claim that the pyramids on Mars were built in the future and sent back in time. A highly visual, large format book, with patents, photos and schematics. Be the first on your block to build your own time travel device!

**316 PAGES. 7x10 PAPERBACK. ILLUSTRATED. $16.95. CODE: TTH**

## ANCIENT ALIENS ON THE MOON
### By Mike Bara
What did NASA find in their explorations of the solar system that they may have kept from the general public? How ancient really are these ruins on the Moon? Using official NASA and Russian photos of the Moon, Bara looks at vast cityscapes and domes in the Sinus Medii region as well as glass domes in the Crisium region. Bara also takes a detailed look at the mission of Apollo 17 and the case that this was a salvage mission, primarily concerned with investigating an opening into a massive hexagonal ruin near the landing site. Chapters include: The History of Lunar Anomalies; The Early 20$^{th}$ Century; Sinus Medii; To the Moon Alice!; Mare Crisium; Yes, Virginia, We Really Went to the Moon; Apollo 17; more. Tons of photos of the Moon examined for possible structures and other anomalies.
**248 Pages. 6x9 Paperback. Illustrated.. $19.95. Code: AAOM**

## ANCIENT ALIENS ON MARS
### By Mike Bara
Bara brings us this lavishly illustrated volume on alien structures on Mars. Was there once a vast, technologically advanced civilization on Mars, and did it leave evidence of its existence behind for humans to find eons later? Did these advanced extraterrestrial visitors vanish in a solar system wide cataclysm of their own making, only to make their way to Earth and start anew? Was Mars once as lush and green as the Earth, and teeming with life? Chapters include: War of the Worlds; The Mars Tidal Model; The Death of Mars; Cydonia and the Face on Mars; The Monuments of Mars; The Search for Life on Mars; The True Colors of Mars and The Pathfinder Sphinx; more. Color section.
**252 Pages. 6x9 Paperback. Illustrated. $19.95. Code: AMAR**

## ANCIENT ALIENS ON MARS II
### By Mike Bara
Using data acquired from sophisticated new scientific instruments like the Mars Odyssey THEMIS infrared imager, Bara shows that the region of Cydonia overlays a vast underground city full of enormous structures and devices that may still be operating. He peels back the layers of mystery to show images of tunnel systems, temples and ruins, and exposes the sophisticated NASA conspiracy designed to hide them. Bara also tackles the enigma of Mars' hollowed out moon Phobos, and exposes evidence that it is artificial. Long-held myths about Mars, including claims that it is protected by a sophisticated UFO defense system, are examined. Data from the Mars rovers Spirit, Opportunity and Curiosity are examined; everything from fossilized plants to mechanical debris is exposed in images taken directly from NASA's own archives.
**294 Pages. 6x9 Paperback. Illustrated. $19.95. Code: AAM2**

## ANCIENT TECHNOLOGY IN PERU & BOLIVIA
### By David Hatcher Childress
Childress speculates on the existence of a sunken city in Lake Titicaca and reveals new evidence that the Sumerians may have arrived in South America 4,000 years ago. He demonstrates that the use of "keystone cuts" with metal clamps poured into them to secure megalithic construction was an advanced technology used all over the world, from the Andes to Egypt, Greece and Southeast Asia. He maintains that only power tools could have made the intricate articulation and drill holes found in extremely hard granite and basalt blocks in Bolivia and Peru, and that the megalith builders had to have had advanced methods for moving and stacking gigantic blocks of stone, some weighing over 100 tons.
**340 Pages. 6x9 Paperback. Illustrated.. $19.95 Code: ATP**

## ROSWELL AND THE REICH
### The Nazi Connection
### By Joseph P. Farrell

Farrell has meticulously reviewed the best-known Roswell research from UFO-ET advocates and skeptics alike, as well as some little-known source material, and comes to a radically different scenario of what happened in Roswell, New Mexico in July 1947, and why the US military has continued to cover it up to this day. Farrell presents a fascinating case sure to disturb both ET believers and disbelievers, namely, that what crashed may have been representative of an independent postwar Nazi power—an extraterritorial Reich monitoring its old enemy, America, and the continuing development of the very technologies confiscated from Germany at the end of the War.
**540 pages. 6x9 Paperback. Illustrated. $19.95. Code: RWR**

## SECRETS OF THE UNIFIED FIELD
### The Philadelphia Experiment, the Nazi Bell, and the Discarded Theory
### by Joseph P. Farrell

Farrell examines the now discarded Unified Field Theory. American and German wartime scientists and engineers determined that, while the theory was incomplete, it could nevertheless be engineered. Chapters include: The Meanings of "Torsion"; Wringing an Aluminum Can; The Mistake in Unified Field Theories and Their Discarding by Contemporary Physics; Three Routes to the Doomsday Weapon: Quantum Potential, Torsion, and Vortices; Tesla's Meeting with FDR; Arnold Sommerfeld and Electromagnetic Radar Stealth; Electromagnetic Phase Conjugations, Phase Conjugate Mirrors, and Templates; The Unified Field Theory, the Torsion Tensor, and Igor Witkowski's Idea of the Plasma Focus; tons more.
**340 pages. 6x9 Paperback. Illustrated. $18.95. Code: SOUF**

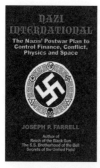

## NAZI INTERNATIONAL
### The Nazi's Postwar Plan to Control Finance, Conflict, Physics and Space
### by Joseph P. Farrell

Beginning with prewar corporate partnerships in the USA, including some with the Bush family, he moves on to the surrender of Nazi Germany, and evacuation plans of the Germans. He then covers the vast, and still-little-known recreation of Nazi Germany in South America with help of Juan Peron, I.G. Farben and Martin Bormann. Farrell then covers Nazi Germany's penetration of the Muslim world including Wilhelm Voss and Otto Skorzeny in Gamel Abdul Nasser's Egypt before moving on to the development and control of new energy technologies including the Bariloche Fusion Project, Dr. Philo Farnsworth's Plasmator.
**412 pages. 6x9 Paperback. Illustrated. $19.95. Code: NZIN**

## MASS CONTROL
### Engineering Human Consciousness
### by Jim Keith

Conspiracy expert Keith's final book on mind control, Project Monarch, and mass manipulation presents chilling evidence that we are indeed spinning a Matrix. Keith describes the New Man, where conception of reality is a dance of electronic images fired into his forebrain, a gossamer construction of his masters, designed so that he will not perceive the actual. His happiness is delivered to him through a tube or an electronic connection. His God lurks behind an electronic curtain; when the curtain is pulled away we find the CIA sorcerer, the media manipulator... Chapters on the CIA, Tavistock, Jolly West and the Violence Center, Guerrilla Mindwar, Brice Taylor, other recent "victims," more.
**256 Pages. 6x9 Paperback. Illustrated. $16.95. code: MASC**

## ANCIENT ALIENS & SECRET SOCIETIES
### By Mike Bara

Did ancient "visitors"—of extraterrestrial origin—come to Earth long, long ago and fashion man in their own image? Were the science and secrets that they taught the ancients intended to be a guide for all humanity to the present era? Bara establishes the reality of the catastrophe that jolted the human race, and traces the history of secret societies from the priesthood of Amun in Egypt to the Templars in Jerusalem and the Scottish Rite Freemasons. Bara also reveals the true origins of NASA and exposes the bizarre triad of secret societies in control of that agency since its inception. Chapters include: Out of the Ashes; From the Sky Down; Ancient Aliens?; The Dawn of the Secret Societies; The Fractures of Time; Into the 20th Century; The Wink of an Eye; more.

**288 Pages. 6x9 Paperback. Illustrated. $19.95. Code: AASS**

## THE CRYSTAL SKULLS
### Astonishing Portals to Man's Past
### by David Hatcher Childress and Stephen S. Mehler

Childress introduces the technology and lore of crystals, and then plunges into the turbulent times of the Mexican Revolution form the backdrop for the rollicking adventures of Ambrose Bierce, the renowned journalist who went missing in the jungles in 1913, and F.A. Mitchell-Hedges, the notorious adventurer who emerged from the jungles with the most famous of the crystal skulls. Mehler shares his extensive knowledge of and experience with crystal skulls. Having been involved in the field since the 1980s, he has personally examined many of the most influential skulls, and has worked with the leaders in crystal skull research, including the inimitable Nick Nocerino, who developed a meticulous methodology for the purpose of examining the skulls.

**294 pages. 6x9 Paperback. Illustrated. Bibliography. $18.95. Code: CRSK**

## AXIS OF THE WORLD
### The Search for the Oldest American Civilization
### by Igor Witkowski

Polish author Witkowski's research reveals remnants of a high civilization that was able to exert its influence on almost the entire planet, and did so with full consciousness. Sites around South America show that this was not just one of the places influenced by this culture, but a place where they built their crowning achievements. Easter Island, in the southeastern Pacific, constitutes one of them. The Rongo-Rongo language that developed there points westward to the Indus Valley. Taken together, the facts presented by Witkowski provide a fresh, new proof that an antediluvian, great civilization flourished several millennia ago.

**220 pages. 6x9 Paperback. Illustrated. References. $18.95. Code: AXOW**

## LEY LINE & EARTH ENERGIES
### An Extraordinary Journey into the Earth's Natural Energy System
### by David Cowan & Chris Arnold

The mysterious standing stones, burial grounds and stone circles that lace Europe, the British Isles and other areas have intrigued scientists, writers, artists and travellers through the centuries. How do ley lines work? How did our ancestors use Earth energy to map their sacred sites and burial grounds? How do ghosts and poltergeists interact with Earth energy? How can Earth spirals and black spots affect our health? This exploration shows how natural forces affect our behavior, how they can be used to enhance our health and well being.

**368 PAGES. 6x9 PAPERBACK. ILLUSTRATED. $18.95. CODE: LLEE**

## SAUCERS, SWASTIKAS AND PSYOPS
### A History of a Breakaway Civilization
### By Joseph P. Farrell

Farrell discusses SS Commando Otto Skorzeny; George Adamski; the alleged Hannebu and Vril craft of the Third Reich; The Strange Case of Dr. Hermann Oberth; Nazis in the US and their connections to "UFO contactees"; The Memes—an idea or behavior spread from person to person within a culture—are Implants. Chapters include: The Nov. 20, 1952 Contact: The Memes are Implants; The Interplanetary Federation of Brotherhood; Adamski's Technological Descriptions and Another ET Message: The Danger of Weaponized Gravity; Adamski's Retro-Looking Saucers, and the Nazi Saucer Myth; Dr. Oberth's 1968 Statements on UFOs and Extraterrestrials; more.
**272 Pages. 6x9 Paperback. Illustrated. $19.95. Code: SSPY**

## LBJ AND THE CONSPIRACY TO KILL KENNEDY
### By Joseph P. Farrell

Farrell says that a coalescence of interests in the military industrial complex, the CIA, and Lyndon Baines Johnson's powerful and corrupt political machine in Texas led to the events culminating in the assassination of JFK. Chapters include: Oswald, the FBI, and the CIA: Hoover's Concern of a Second Oswald; Oswald and the Anti-Castro Cubans; The Mafia; Hoover, Johnson, and the Mob; The FBI, the Secret Service, Hoover, and Johnson; The CIA and "Murder Incorporated"; Ruby's Bizarre Behavior; The French Connection and Permindex; Big Oil; The Dead Witnesses: Guy Bannister, Jr., Mary Pinchot Meyer, Rose Cheramie, Dorothy Killgallen, Congressman Hale Boggs; LBJ and the Planning of the Texas Trip; LBJ: A Study in Character, Connections, and Cabals; LBJ and the Aftermath: Accessory After the Fact; The Requirements of Coups D'État; more.
**342 Pages. 6x9 Paperback. $19.95 Code: LCKK**

## THE TESLA PAPERS
### Nikola Tesla on Free Energy &
### Wireless Transmission of Power
### by Nikola Tesla, edited by David Hatcher Childress

David Hatcher Childress takes us into the incredible world of Nikola Tesla and his amazing inventions. Tesla's fantastic vision of the future, including wireless power, anti-gravity, free energy and highly advanced solar power. Also included are some of the papers, patents and material collected on Tesla at the Colorado Springs Tesla Symposiums, including papers on: •The Secret History of Wireless Transmission •Tesla and the Magnifying Transmitter •Design and Construction of a Half-Wave Tesla Coil •Electrostatics: A Key to Free Energy •Progress in Zero-Point Energy Research •Electromagnetic Energy from Antennas to Atoms
**325 PAGES. 8x10 PAPERBACK. ILLUSTRATED. $16.95. CODE: TTP**

## COVERT WARS & THE CLASH OF CIVILIZATIONS
### UFOs, Oligarchs and Space Secrecy
### By Joseph P. Farrell

Farrell's customary meticulous research and sharp analysis blow the lid off of a worldwide web of nefarious financial and technological control that very few people even suspect exists. He elaborates on the advanced technology that they took with them at the "end" of World War II and shows how the breakaway civilizations have created a huge system of hidden finance with the involvement of various banks and financial institutions around the world. He investigates the current space secrecy that involves UFOs, suppressed technologies and the hidden oligarchs who control planet earth for their own gain and profit.
**358 Pages. 6x9 Paperback. Illustrated. $19.95. Code: CWCC**

## HITLER'S SUPPRESSED AND STILL-SECRET WEAPONS, SCIENCE AND TECHNOLOGY
### by Henry Stevens
In the closing months of WWII the Allies assembled mind-blowing intelligence reports of supermetals, electric guns, and ray weapons able to stop the engines of Allied aircraft—in addition to feared x-ray and laser weaponry. Chapters include: The Kammler Group; German Flying Disc Update; The Electromagnetic Vampire; Liquid Air; Synthetic Blood; German Free Energy Research; German Atomic Tests; The Fuel-Air Bomb; Supermetals; Red Mercury; Means to Stop Engines; more.
**335 Pages. 6x9 Paperback. Illustrated. $19.95. Code: HSSW**

## PRODIGAL GENIUS
### The Life of Nikola Tesla
### by John J. O'Neill
This special edition of O'Neill's book has many rare photographs of Tesla and his most advanced inventions. Tesla's eccentric personality gives his life story a strange romantic quality. He made his first million before he was forty, yet gave up his royalties in a gesture of friendship, and died almost in poverty. Tesla could see an invention in 3-D, from every angle, within his mind, before it was built; how he refused to accept the Nobel Prize; his friendships with Mark Twain, George Westinghouse and competition with Thomas Edison. Tesla is revealed as a figure of genius whose influence on the world reaches into the far future. Deluxe, illustrated edition.
**408 pages. 6x9 Paperback. Illustrated. Bibliography. $18.95. Code: PRG**

## HAARP
### The Ultimate Weapon of the Conspiracy
### by Jerry Smith
The HAARP project in Alaska is one of the most controversial projects ever undertaken by the U.S. Government. At at worst, HAARP could be the most dangerous device ever created, a futuristic technology that is everything from super-beam weapon to world-wide mind control device. Topics include Over-the-Horizon Radar and HAARP, Mind Control, ELF and HAARP, The Telsa Connection, The Russian Woodpecker, GWEN & HAARP, Earth Penetrating Tomography, Weather Modification, Secret Science of the Conspiracy, more. Includes the complete 1987 Eastlund patent for his pulsed super-weapon that he claims was stolen by the HAARP Project.
**256 pages. 6x9 Paperback. Illustrated. Bib. $14.95. Code: HARP**

## WEATHER WARFARE
### The Military's Plan to Draft Mother Nature
### by Jerry E. Smith
Weather modification in the form of cloud seeding to increase snow packs in the Sierras or suppress hail over Kansas is now an everyday affair. Underground nuclear tests in Nevada have set off earthquakes. A Russian company has been offering to sell typhoons (hurricanes) on demand since the 1990s. Scientists have been searching for ways to move hurricanes for over fifty years. In the same amount of time we went from the Wright Brothers to Neil Armstrong. Hundreds of environmental and weather modifying technologies have been patented in the United States alone – and hundreds more are being developed in civilian, academic, military and quasi-military laboratories around the world *at this moment!* Numerous ongoing military programs do inject aerosols at high altitude for communications and surveillance operations.
**304 Pages. 6x9 Paperback. Illustrated. Bib. $18.95. Code: WWAR**

# ORDER FORM

**10% Discount When You Order 3 or More Items!**

One Adventure Place
P.O. Box 74
Kempton, Illinois 60946
United States of America
Tel.: 815-253-6390 • Fax: 815-253-6300
Email: auphq@frontiernet.net
http://www.adventuresunlimitedpress.com

## ORDERING INSTRUCTIONS

✓ Remit by USD$ Check, Money Order or Credit Card

✓ Visa, Master Card, Discover & AmEx Accepted

✓ Paypal Payments Can Be Made To:

    info@wexclub.com

✓ Prices May Change Without Notice

✓ 10% Discount for 3 or More Items

## SHIPPING CHARGES

### United States

✓ Postal Book Rate { $4.50 First Item / 50¢ Each Additional Item

✓ POSTAL BOOK RATE Cannot Be Tracked!
    Not responsible for non-delivery.

✓ Priority Mail { $6.00 First Item / $2.00 Each Additional Item

✓ UPS { $7.00 First Item / $1.50 Each Additional Item

    NOTE: UPS Delivery Available to Mainland USA Only

### Canada

✓ Postal Air Mail { $15.00 First Item / $2.50 Each Additional Item

✓ Personal Checks or Bank Drafts MUST BE

    US$ and Drawn on a US Bank

✓ Canadian Postal Money Orders OK

✓ Payment MUST BE US$

### All Other Countries

✓ Sorry, No Surface Delivery!

✓ Postal Air Mail { $19.00 First Item / $6.00 Each Additional Item

✓ Checks and Money Orders MUST BE US$
    and Drawn on a US Bank or branch.

✓ Paypal Payments Can Be Made in US$ To:
    info@wexclub.com

## SPECIAL NOTES

✓ RETAILERS: Standard Discounts Available

✓ BACKORDERS: We Backorder all Out-of-
    Stock Items Unless Otherwise Requested

✓ PRO FORMA INVOICES: Available on Request

✓ DVD Return Policy: Replace defective DVDs only

ORDER ONLINE AT: www.adventuresunlimitedpress.com

**10% Discount When You Order 3 or More Items!**

---

*Please check:* ✓

☐ This is my first order    ☐ I have ordered before

Name

Address

City

State/Province      Postal Code

Country

Phone: Day      Evening

Fax      Email

| Item Code | Item Description | Qty | Total |
|---|---|---|---|
| | | | |
| | | | |
| | | | |
| | | | |
| | | | |
| | | | |
| | | | |
| | | | |
| | | | |
| | | | |
| | | | |
| | | | |
| | | | |

*Please check:* ✓

| | Subtotal ▶ | |
|---|---|---|
| | Less Discount-10% for 3 or more items ▶ | |
| ☐ Postal-Surface | Balance ▶ | |
| ☐ Postal-Air Mail (Priority in USA) | Illinois Residents 6.25% Sales Tax ▶ | |
| | Previous Credit ▶ | |
| ☐ UPS | Shipping ▶ | |
| (Mainland USA only) | Total (check/MO in USD$ only) ▶ | |

☐ Visa/MasterCard/Discover/American Express

Card Number:

Expiration Date:      Security Code:

✓ SEND A CATALOG TO A FRIEND: